Praise for *A Fearless Heart*

"*A* ... is a rare book that shows how the meeting of contemplative insights and practices with modern science can lead to offerings that are beneficial for everyone interested in deeper personal spiritual transformation. The book shows how such practices can have a positive impact in our daily lives. I applaud my long-time English translator Thupten Jinpa for writing this timely book on compassion and its cultivation."

The Dalai Lama

"I love Jinpa's sense of the practical, of bringing compassion down from the pedestal of high ideals and into the messy reality that is everyday human life. *A Fearless Heart* may prove to be one of the important books of these difficult times."

Richard Gere

"Firmly grounded in the latest scientific studies, and hugely invitational and convincing in its inspiration, its reasoning, its heartfulness, and its guidance in a broad range of powerful practices, *A Fearless Heart* is the bravest, clearest, and most engaging book I know on why we need to *cultivate* compassion, and on how to bring it more widely and deeply into our lives and into the world."

Jon Kabat-Zinn, Founder of Mindfulness-based Stress Reduction and author of *Full Catastrophe Living*

"Thupten Jinpa speaks from his expertise as a monk turned family man, and a topflight scholar, who draws on his remarkable background and range of knowledge to offer each one of us a practical toolkit for becoming a better human being. *A Fearless Heart* can help anyone nurture the compassion that lies within every heart."

Daniel Goleman, author of *Emotional Intelligence*

"Brilliantly clear and heartfelt, a potentially life-changing work offering inspiring training. *A Fearless Heart* is personally moving, eminently practical and visionary in scope."

Jack Kornfield, author of *The Wise Heart*

"Jinpa shows why compassion is not a given within some yet not possible for others, but rather is a quality of the heart that we all can cultivate and expand. If we do that, our lives transform, our families and relationships transform, and our world transforms."

Sharon Salzberg, author of *Loving Kindness* and *Real Happiness*

"Part autobiography, part a training manual for a wholesome life and part a beautiful tapestry woven between ancient Buddhist thought and modern science, this book has something for everyone. At its fundamental core, it makes the case for why compassion is so essential for the modern world and offers detailed helpful advice on how it can be cultivated."

Richard J. Davidson, co-author of *The Emotional Life of Your Brain*; Founder, Center for Investigating Healthy Minds, University of Wisconsin-Madison

"As I read *A Fearless Heart*, I began picturing the possibilities that await us if we safeguard our children's natural instinct for kindness. Filled with wise insights, research and anecdotes, Jinpa lays out a path for living with compassion and acceptance, both for others, and for ourselves. An essential guide for anyone committed to creating a loving, peaceful world, but a must-read for parents, whose simple interactions with their children will lead to a quiet revolution toward a compassionate world."

Susan Stiffelman, author of *Parenting with Presence: Practices for Raising Conscious, Confident, Caring Kids*

"An inspirational read that not only demonstrates the power of compassion, but also reveals how kindness and self-compassion are within our reach."

Kelly McGonigal, author of *The Upside of Stress* and *The Willpower Instinct*

"Embracing compassion enables us to step into our own natural capacity for creativity and empathy. I highly recommend this extraordinary book and this path to anyone who seeks to have more meaningful connections to people and the world."

David Kelley, Founder of IDEO and co-author of *Creative Confidence: Unleashing the Creative Potential Within Us All*

A Fearless Heart

THUPTEN JINPA

piatkus

PIATKUS

First published in the US in 2015 by Penguin Group USA
First published in Great Britain in 2015 by Piatkus
This paperback edition published in 2017 by Piatkus

1 3 5 7 9 10 8 6 4 2

Copyright © 2015 by Thupten Jinpa

The moral right of the author has been asserted.

A CIP catalogue record for this book
is available from the British Library.

ISBN 978-0-349-40627-5

Typeset in Stone Serif by M Rules
Printed and bound in Great Britain by
Clays Ltd, St Ives plc

Papers used by Piatkus are from well-managed forests
and other responsible sources.

Piatkus
An imprint of
Carmelite House
50 Victoria Embankment
London EC4Y 0DZ

An Hachette UK Company
www.hachette.co.uk

www.theimprovementzone.co.uk

To my late parents, who despite all their hardships
as Tibetan refugees in India, instilled in me
faith in the basic goodness of humanity

About the Author

A former Tibetan monk, Thupten Jinpa holds a PhD from Cambridge University and has been the principal English translator to the Dalai Lama for nearly thirty years. He is an adjunct professor at the Faculty of Religious Studies at McGill University, Montreal, and chairman of the Mind and Life Institute, which is dedicated to promoting collaboration between the sciences and contemplative knowledge, especially Buddhism. Jinpa helped develop the groundbreaking and highly regarded Compassion Cultivation Training (CCT) course at Stanford University School of Medicine.

Contents

2 The Key to Self-Acceptance:
Having Compassion for Yourself 51

3 From Fear to Courage:
Breaking Through Our Resistance 72

PART II: TRAINING OUR MIND AND HEART

4 From Compassion to Action:
Turning Intention into Motivation 95

5 Making Way for Compassion:
How Focused Awareness Keeps Us on Track 115

6 Getting Unstuck: Escaping the Prison of Excessive Self-Involvement 140

7 "May I Be Happy": Caring for Ourselves 162

8 "Just Like Me": Expanding Our Circle of Concern 184

PART III A NEW WAY OF BEING

9 Greater Well-being: How Compassion Makes Us Healthy and Strong   213

10 More Courage, Less Stress, Greater Freedom: Making Compassion Our Basic Stance   229

11 The Power of One:
The Way to a More Compassionate World   247

A
Fearless
Heart

Introduction

Nothing is more powerful than an idea whose time has come.

—Victor Hugo

I remember walking excitedly next to His Holiness the Dalai Lama, holding his hand and trying to keep up with his pace. I must have been about six when the Dalai Lama visited the Stirling Castle Home for Tibetan Children in Shimla, northern India. I was one of more than two hundred children of refugees resident there. The home was set up by the British charity Save the Children in 1962 in two former British colonial homes located on a small hill. We children had been busy preparing for the visit, rehearsing welcoming Tibetan songs while the grown-ups swept the road and decorated it with Tibetan symbols in white lime powder—lotus, infinite knot, vase, two goldfish (facing each other), eight-spoke wheel of dharma, victory banner, parasol, and conch. The day the Dalai Lama came, there were many Indian policemen around the school; I remember playing marbles with a few of them that morning while we waited. When the moment finally arrived it was magical. Thick smoke billowed from a whitewashed incense stove built especially for the occasion. Dressed in our colorful best and holding *kata*, the traditional Tibetan white scarves of greeting, in our hands, we stood on both sides of the driveway leading up to the school and sang at the top of our lungs.

I had been chosen as one of the students to walk alongside the Dalai Lama as he toured the school. While we walked, I asked him if I could become a monk, to which he replied, "Study well and you can become a monk anytime you wish." Looking back, I think the only reason I was so precociously attracted to being a monk was because there were two monk teachers at the children's home. They were the kindest of the adults there and also seemed the most learned. They always looked happy and at peace, even radiant at times. Most important for us children, they told the most interesting stories.

So when the first opportunity came, at the age of eleven— and as it happened, on the first day of Tibetan New Year (toward the end of February, that year)—I became a monk and joined a monastery, despite my father's protestations. He was upset that I was squandering the opportunity to become the family breadwinner—parents of his generation wished for their children to get an education and work in an office. For nearly a decade afterward, I lived, worked, meditated, chanted, and belonged in the small community of Dzongkar Choede monastery. It was there in the quiet evergreen hills of Dharamsala, northern India, that I practiced my rudimentary English with enlightenment-seeking hippies.

I developed friendships with John and Lars. John was not a hippie. He was an American recluse who lived alone in a nice bungalow he'd rented close to the meditation hut of a revered Tibetan master. I met with John once or twice a week. We would speak and I would read from a Tibetan text, which itself is a translation of an eighth-century Indian Buddhist classic. It was John who introduced me to pancakes and ham.

Lars was a Danish man who lived quite close to the monastery. Often I would visit him to chat and have toast with jam.

In the spring of 1972, the monastery moved to the scorching heat of southern India, where a Tibetan resettlement program had begun. There, like the other monks of my monastery, at the age of thirteen, I joined the resettlement workforce clearing forests, digging ditches, and working in the cornfields. For the first two years, while the settlement was being prepared, we were paid a daily wage of 0.75 Indian rupees.

There was very little formal education at Dzongkar Choede. It's not the custom for young monks to go to regular secular schools either. By the time our community moved to South India, I had finished memorizing all the liturgical texts that were required. The day's labor at the settlement finished by four in the afternoon, so I had some free time on my hands and I decided to pick up my English again. However, with no opportunities to practice conversation, I made do with reading comic books. One day, I obtained a cheap used transistor radio, and after that I listened to the BBC World Service and U. S.-based Voice of America every day. In those days, VOA had a unique program "broadcasting in special English," in which the presenter spoke slowly and repeated every sentence twice. This was immensely helpful, as I had only a very basic grasp of the language at the time.

Since I was the only young boy at the monastery who could speak and read English, rudimentarily though it was at first, it was a source of pride and also a way of individuating myself from the others. Here was a world—figuratively and literally the whole world beyond the refugee community, beyond the monastery—that I alone from my monastic community could enter. Through English I learned to read the globe, which made all the great countries I was hearing about in the news come to life—England, America, Russia, and, of course, our beloved Tibet, which had tragically fallen to Communist China.

Around 1976, when I was seventeen or eighteen, I met a remarkable woman who changed my karma with English. Dr. Valentina Stache-Rosen was a German Indologist with expertise in Sanskrit and Chinese texts, living in Bangalore (where her husband headed the Max Muller Institute). Dr. Stache-Rosen took a keen interest in the progress of my English. She introduced me to Western literature and sent me books— Hermann Hesse and Agatha Christie, Edgar Snow's *Red Star over China*, and, most helpfully, a large English dictionary with many examples of words used in sentences. And I first learned to use a knife and fork at Dr. Stache-Rosen's home. We corresponded until her death in 1980. Without her kindness, I can't imagine how my English would have escaped from where it remained back then, or for that matter, where my life would have taken me.

I also read Trevor Ling's book *The Buddha*, a portrayal, written in English, of the life and teachings of the Buddha as a revolutionary, philosopher, and spiritual teacher. In this book in particular, the evocative power of the English language deeply impressed me. There was a liveliness and immediacy that I had never felt with written Tibetan; it was like someone speaking. (The gap between written and spoken language in Tibetan is huge.)

Around the same time, I met the Tibetan teacher who later became one of the most important influences on my classical Buddhist education. Famed for his erudition and poetry, Zemey Rinpoche was the gentlest person I have ever known. He was living a semiretired life then, dedicated to quiet meditative reflection, in another Tibetan settlement about an hour's bus ride from my monastery. I was already familiar with Rinpoche's name from the many Tibetan language school textbooks he had edited. Meeting him in person and speaking with him rekindled the enthusiasm for learning that had originally inspired me to become a monk. From our first meeting, Rinpoche recognized my restless intellect and took me under his wing. So, in the summer of 1978, I left my small monastery to join Ganden, a large academic monastery in another part of southern India, about a ten- to twelve-hour bus ride away.

In 1985, while on a visit to Dharamsala, North India, twenty years after I'd hurried to keep up with His Holiness as a small boy, I had the wonderful, if accidental, honor of being asked to interpret at a teaching given by the Dalai Lama when the scheduled English interpreter couldn't make it on the first day. A few days into the teaching, the Dalai Lama's office informed me that His Holiness wished to see me. At the appointed time, the secretary ushered me into the audience room that is part of the Dalai Lama's office complex, a simple colonial-style bungalow of stone and wood with a green corrugated tin roof. As I entered, His Holiness said, "I know you; you are a good debater at Ganden monastery. But I did not know you spoke English." Some Westerners who had listened to my interpreting had told the Dalai Lama that my English was easy to listen to. His Holiness asked me if I could be available when he needed someone to interpret for him, especially on his travels. I was in tears. I had never, even in a dream, imagined that one day I would have the honor of serving the Dalai Lama so closely. Needless to say, I replied that this would be the greatest honor.

For a Tibetan who grew up as a refugee in India, serving the Dalai Lama—so deeply revered by the Tibetan people—is also a way to honor the sacrifices our parents had to make in their early years of exile.

So I began accompanying the Dalai Lama on his international travels, interpreting for him with English-speaking audiences and colleagues in the multidisciplinary field of contemplative studies, including major scientific meetings like the Mind and Life Dialogues,[1] and assisting him on his book projects. In these capacities, I have been the Dalai Lama's principal English translator since 1985, serving this remarkable voice of compassion for nearly three decades now.

Right from the beginning His Holiness was clear that I would not join his permanent staff. He said that this would be a waste of my monastic education and talent. He advised me instead to concentrate on my studies and pursue an independent life dedicated to scholarship. This was truly compassionate.

Over time I came to recognize that my personal destiny might lie in serving as a medium for my own classical Tibetan Buddhist tradition in the contemporary world. Perhaps the strange background of my youth—growing up in a monastery yet with a fascination for the English language and things Western—had prepared me for this role. There weren't many people trained in the classical Buddhist tradition who also knew English then. As my facility with English improved, it dawned on me that I might have a special role to play at the interface of two cultures I loved.

The motivation to fulfill this destiny more efficiently took me to Cambridge University, in England, beginning a new phase in my life. Thanks to the kindness of so many people, I have been fortunate to be able to dedicate my professional life to being such a medium of cultural interchange, whether through serving the Dalai Lama or translating key Tibetan texts into English. My experiences have confirmed that early intuition that a lot of good could come from the meeting of classical Tibetan Buddhist tradition and contemporary thought and culture, including science. This book is part of this larger work of cross-cultural interpretation.

I have been interested in compassion my whole life. In my childhood, I was at the receiving end of other people's compassion. Thanks to thousands of ordinary British citizens who contributed to Save the Children, more than a thousand Tibetan children like me found a home to grow up in safely in the early 1960s, while our parents struggled to adjust as refugees in a land where they did not speak the language or know the customs. Thanks to individuals such as Dr. Valentina Stache-Rosen and Zemey Rinpoche, I found a purpose as I struggled through my very unconventional education. In my professional life, serving the Dalai Lama so closely, I have had the privilege of witnessing, from the front seat as it were, what it means for someone to live a life with complete conviction in this defining human quality we call compassion.

Today I am a husband and a father of two teenage daughters. I live in a North American city and lead a life very different from the one I was used to in a Tibetan monastery in India. On a daily basis, I struggle like most people with the typical challenges of a fast-paced modern life—balancing work, family, and relationships, paying the bills—while maintaining sanity, a sense of proportion, and basic optimism. Remarkably, it's in the teachings of my own Tibetan Buddhist tradition that I find many of the tools that help me navigate the challenges of everyday living in the contemporary world. I hope to share some of these in this book.

What is compassion? Most of us value compassion and agree that it is important both in our own lives as well as in society more generally. Undeniably, compassion is also part of our everyday experience of being human. We love and care for our children; confronted with someone in pain, we instinctively feel for that person; when someone reaches out to us in a time of distress we feel touched. Most of us would also agree that compassion has something to do with what it means to lead a good life. So it's no small coincidence that compassion turns out to be the common ground where the ethical teachings of all major traditions, religious and humanistic, come together. Even in the contested political arena, compassion is one value that both sides of the spectrum are eager to claim.

Despite our widely shared experience and beliefs about compassion, we fail to give it a central role in our lives and in our society. In our contemporary culture, we tend to have a rather confused relationship with values like kindness and compassion. In the secular West, we lack a coherent cultural framework for articulating what compassion is and how it works. To some people, it's a matter of religion and morality, a private concern of the individual with little or no societal relevance. Others question the very possibility of selflessness for human beings, and are suspicious of sentiments like compassion that have other people's welfare as the primary concern. As a well-known scientist once remarked, "Scratch an altruist and watch a hypocrite bleed."[2] At the other extreme, some people elevate these qualities to such heights that they are out of reach for most of us, possible only for exceptional individuals like Mother Teresa, Nelson Mandela, and the Dalai Lama. Compassion then becomes something to be admired at a distance in great beings, but not relevant to our everyday lives.

Broadly defined, compassion is *a sense of concern that arises when we are confronted with another's suffering and feel motivated to see that suffering relieved.* The English word *compassion*, from its Latin root, literally means "to suffer with." According to religious historian Karen Armstrong, the word for *compassion* in Semitic languages—*rahamanut* in Hebrew and *rahman* in Arabic—is etymologically related to the word for womb, evoking the mother's love for her child as an archetypal expression of our compassion.[3] At its core, compassion is a response to the inevitable reality of our human condition—our experience of pain and sorrow.

Compassion offers the possibility of responding to suffering with understanding, patience, and kindness rather than, say, fear and repulsion. As such, compassion lets us open ourselves to the reality of suffering and seek its alleviation. Compassion is what connects the feeling of empathy to acts of kindness, generosity, and other expressions of our altruistic tendencies.

When compassion arises in us in the face of need or suffering, three things happen almost instantaneously: We perceive the other's suffering or need; we emotionally connect with that need or suffering; and we respond instinctively by wishing to see that situation relieved. Compassion may lead to action; it is a readiness to help or to want to do something ourselves about another person's situation. Today, scientists are beginning to map the neurobiological basis of compassion and explore its deep evolutionary roots.[4]

As a society, we have long ignored the fundamental role our compassion instinct plays in defining our nature and behavior. We have bought into a popular narrative that seeks to explain all our behavior through the prism of competition and self-interest. This is the story we have been telling about ourselves.

The thing about a story like this is that it tends to be self-fulfilling. When our story says that we are at heart selfish and aggressive creatures, we assume that every man *is* for himself. In this "dog eat dog world" it is only logical, then, to see others as a source of rivalry and antagonism. And so we relate to others with apprehension, fear, and suspicion, instead of with fellow feeling and a sense of connection. By contrast, if our story says that we are social creatures endowed with instincts for compassion and kindness, and that as deeply interdependent beings our welfare is intertwined, this totally changes the way we view—and behave in—the world. So the stories we tell about ourselves do matter, quite profoundly so.

Why compassion now?

Today several forces are converging that indicate that compassion's time has come. As our world becomes smaller—with our population rapidly increasing against finite natural resources; environmental problems that affect us all; and the proximity of peoples, cultures, and religions brought about by technology, demographic changes, and a global economy—we are being urgently called to foster the spirit of coexistence and cooperation. We actually are in this together. This reality of the oneness of humankind is what compassion is all about. If, for example, the world's believers collectively reaffirmed compassion as the foundation of their teachings, there would be a robust common ground on which millions of people could come together and respect each other.[5] In a series of moving dialogues with the Dalai Lama, the noted emotion scientist Paul Ekman makes a powerful case that what he calls "global compassion" is the most important challenge of our time.[6] If we, as individuals and together as a global society, can take the compassionate part of our nature seriously, we have a real chance of making a more humane world.

Findings from diverse fields—primate studies, child development psychology, neuroscience, new economics—show that we are not just self-seeking and competitive creatures, but we are caring and cooperative beings as well. This gives us hope. Furthermore, thanks to new brain imaging technologies and the discovery of brain plasticity—how our brain physically changes in response to our environment and experiences throughout our lives—researchers are also beginning to understand how conscious mental training such as meditation affects our brains. Brain imaging studies on long-term meditators by the noted psychologist and neuroscientist Richard Davidson and others have opened new avenues for exploring the effects of meditation at the neuronal level.[7] These developments in science have led to an entire new field called contemplative science, which studies the effects of contemplative practice like meditation on health, cognitive development, emotion regulation, and more. By training our mind, this new field of science tells us, we can literally change our brain.

I remember years ago, at one of the Mind and Life Dialogues at his residence in India, the Dalai Lama threw out a challenge to the scientists who were present. "You scientists," he said, "have done a remarkable job mapping the pathologies of the human mind. But you have done little or no work on the positive qualities like compassion, let alone their potential for cultivation. Contemplative traditions, on the other hand, have developed techniques to train our mind and enhance the positive qualities like compassion. So why not use your powerful tools now to study the effects of these contemplative practices? Once we have better scientific understanding of the effects of these trainings we can then offer some of them to the wider world, not as spiritual practices but as techniques for mental and emotional well-being."

Those were prophetic words, as the remarkable story of mindfulness demonstrates. Mindfulness in the West began with Buddhist meditations—especially of a type developed for lay practice in Burma at the turn of the twentieth century— which some pioneering Buddhist Americans such as Jack

Kornfield and Joseph Goldstein brought back to America in the 1970s after spending years in monasteries in Southeast Asia. The influences of the Burmese-Indian teacher S.N. Goenka and the Zen teacher Thich Nhat Hanh were also key in this movement. In 1979, Jon Kabat-Zinn opened a clinic at University of Massachusetts medical school for people with chronic pain, using a specially developed mindfulness practice.[8] This came to be known as MBSR (mindfulness-based stress reduction). Based on the success of this treatment, Kabat-Zinn wrote *Full Catastrophe Living*, which presented the program and practice with guided meditations on CDs. By the time his second book, *Wherever You Go, There You Are*, came out, the clinical world had taken on mindfulness, trying out its therapeutic potential for all sorts of problems, including stress, chronic pain, and attention deficit disorders.

In the past decade or so, U.S. Department of Health grants related to mindfulness-based intervention studies have increased exponentially, to the tune of tens of millions of dollars. The Dalai Lama's explicit advocacy for adapting Buddhist-based mental training practices for the secular world has also played a significant part in raising awareness of the benefits of mindfulness. Today mindfulness turns up in therapy, in management and leadership training, in schools, and in competitive sports. Phrases such as "mindful parenting," "mindful leadership," "mindful schools," and "mindfulness for stress management" are mainstream. And searching for "mindfulness" in book titles on Amazon calls up more than three thousand books.

The stage is now set for compassion to make the next big impact in our world. There is a growing scientific movement to redefine the place of compassion in our understanding of human nature and behavior. Therapies based on compassion training are showing promise for mental health conditions ranging from social phobia to excessive negative self-judgment, and from post-traumatic stress disorder to eating disorders. Educators are exploring ways to bring kindness and compassion into schools as part of our children's social, emotional, and ethical development. In this context, an opportunity came to me to design a standardized program for secular compassion training known today as compassion cultivation training (CCT).

Compassion Cultivation Training at Stanford

The story of CCT began in the winter of 2007 when I met Jim Doty, a neurosurgeon with an entrepreneurial spirit. Jim wanted to create a forum for professionals of all stripes to scientifically explore altruistic behavior and its underlying motivations, especially compassion. He asked me if I was interested. Was I ever. The result was CCARE, the Center for Compassion and Altruism Research and Education, at Stanford University, which has helped place the study of compassion squarely within established science. As a visiting scholar at Stanford, I helped developed compassion cultivation training.

CCT started as an eight-week program, a weekly two-hour interactive class covering introductory psychology and guided meditation practices to help develop greater awareness and understanding of the dynamics of our thoughts, emotions, and behavior. Participants do "homework" between classes: pre-recorded guided meditations lasting about fifteen minutes at first and increasing to half an hour. In addition, they do informal practices, using the opportunities of everyday life to work with the lessons of that particular week.

You might ask: How effective can meditation practices drawn from traditional Buddhist techniques be once you strip them of their religious elements? My views on this question are straightforward. As a professional translator I have long admired what Ralph Waldo Emerson said about translatability across languages. In a memorable passage in *Society and Solitude*, Emerson wrote, "What is really best in any book is translatable—any real insight or human sentiment."[9] I believe that this principle holds true not just for translation across languages but also for other forms of communication we use to transmit insights into the human condition. If traditional Buddhist compassion practices touch us in fundamental ways that help nurture and develop our better self, clearly these traditional techniques can be translated into forms that we can all understand, no matter our race, religion, or culture. In other words, the deepest and best truths are universal.

Initially, CCT was offered to Stanford undergraduates and the general public living nearby, and we fine-tuned the program based on this early experience. For example, I recognized that the first version of the program relied too heavily on meditation practice, which didn't work so well for people who were not temperamentally inclined to the silent, reflective approach typical of formal sitting. For these people, more active or interactive exercises proved more effective in evoking the mental and emotional states we aimed to cultivate. So, I incorporated non-meditative techniques. Interactive exercises—two people engaging nonjudgmentally, practicing understanding and empathy, for example—and class discussions were especially helpful here.

To make the training more comprehensive I sought the help of several colleagues, especially three remarkable teachers— Kelly McGonigal, a lecturer at Stanford and well-known yoga and meditation teacher; Margaret Cullen, marriage and family therapist and certified mindfulness trainer; and Erika Rosenberg, emotion researcher and meditation teacher. These three colleagues became the first senior teachers of CCT, later joined by Monica Hanson and Leah Weiss. (Leah worked also as the director of compassion education at CCARE.) It was Kelly and Leah who, in consultation with the team, designed a comprehensive teacher training course on CCT. To date, more than a hundred instructors have been formally trained to teach this course. Through them CCT has been offered to a wide range of participants—from Stanford undergraduates to the general public in Palo Alto and the San Francisco Bay Area; from cancer support networks to residential treatment centers for soldiers and ex-military personnel suffering from PTSD (post-traumatic stress disorder); and from a major private health care group in San Diego to the engineers of Google and students at Stanford Business School. I share in this book some of the stories from the field. For those who are interested I provide, in the endnotes, the sources I have used, including the scientific studies cited in the book.

The Dalai Lama once said that he envisions a time when, just as today we accept good diet and exercise as key to physical health, the world will come to recognize the importance of mental care and training for mental health and human flourishing. That time may not be so far away.

About this book

Here is what I'm trying to say: Compassion is fundamental to our basic nature as human beings. Connecting with our compassionate part, nurturing it, and relating to ourselves, others, and the world around us from this place is the key to our happiness as individuals and our societal well-being. Each one of us can take steps to make compassion a central reality of our own lives and our shared world. In Part II of this book, I will show you those steps.

The aim of this book is thus simple *and* ambitious: To redefine compassion as something we can all grasp, and to reposition it in our lives and in our society as something we want to do—not just something we should do. I hope to bring compassion down from the pedestal of a high ideal and make it an active force in the messy reality that is everyday human life. By presenting a systematic training of our mind and heart, this book maps the way to making compassion our basic stance, the very anchor of a happier, less stressful, more fulfilling life and a more stable and peaceful world.

For it's a paradox of compassion that we ourselves are one of its greatest beneficiaries. As we will see in Part I, compassion makes us happier. It gets us out of our usual head full of disappointments, regrets, and worries about ourselves and focused on something bigger. Perhaps counterintuitively, compassion makes us more optimistic, because although it is focused on suffering, it is an energized state concerned with the ultimately positive wish for the end of suffering as well as the possibility of doing something about it. Compassion gives us a sense of purpose beyond our habitual petty obsessions. It lightens our heart and lifts our stress. It makes us more patient with and understanding of ourselves and others. It gives our minds an alternative to anger and other reactive states, which has been shown to be particularly helpful for military veterans with PTSD. And compassion makes us less lonely and less afraid. Also, in a nice twist, compassion makes us benefit more from other people's kindness toward us.

One CCT participant, a thirty-two-year-old doctor at a busy outpatient clinic, described how compassion helped her:

"I sometimes see thirty-five patients a day. I stopped feeling connected with my patients. They seemed to have become just numbers. I was feeling totally burned out and over- whelmed. I was even thinking of quitting medicine. After I took CCT and began compassion practice, things began to change for me. I changed. I started using the three deep breaths before entering the exam room and in my head I did not take the last patient into the room with me. Somehow I could pay attention to just the person in the room. The suf- fering of the patient before me began to matter again. More important I realized I could give that person my caring besides writing them a prescription. My workday is still too busy and there are too many demands, but I feel less stressed. It feels like what I do has meaning again and I feel more balanced. I intend to keep practicing medicine and compassion."[10]

I celebrate the fact that, as humans, we are never quite free from the dictates of compassion. We were born at the mercy of someone else's care. We grew up and survived into adulthood because we received care from others. Even at the height of our autonomy as adults, the presence or absence of others' affection powerfully defines our happiness or misery. This is human nature—we're vulnerable, and it's a good thing. A fearless heart embraces this fundamental truth of our human condition. We can develop the courage to see and be more compassionately in the world, to live our lives with our hearts wide open to the pain—and joy—of being human on this planet. As utterly social and moral creatures, we each yearn to be recognized and valued. We long to matter, especially in the lives of those whom we love. We like to believe that our existence serves a purpose. We are "meaning-seeking" creatures. It's through connecting with other people, actually making a difference to others, and bringing joy into their lives that we make our own lives matter, that we bring worth and purpose to our lives. This is the power of compassion.

Part I

Why Compassion Matters

1

The Best Kept Secret of Happiness
Compassion

What is that one thing, which when you possess, you have all other virtues? It's compassion.

—Attributed to the Buddha

What wisdom can you find that is greater than kindness?

—Jean-Jacques Rousseau (1712–78)

My mother died when I was nine. I was then at a Tibetan refugee boarding school in Shimla. My parents were part of a large number of refugees—more than eighty thousand—who fled Tibet in the wake of the Dalai Lama's escape to India in 1959. Many of the Tibetans, including my parents, ended up in road construction camps in northern India. With Tibet now annexed by the People's Republic of China, India suddenly needed to defend an international border more than two thousand miles long. Hence the urgent need for new roads. The refugees newly arrived from Tibet were the perfect labor force to take on this challenge of high-altitude road building. My parents worked on the road from the picturesque hill station of Shimla, a town that sits at an altitude above 6,500 feet, to the mountainous Tibetan border. Despite the physical hardships, moving camp every few months as the road progressed, and being separated from their children much of the time, my parents succeeded in creating fond memories of early childhood for me. I still feel warm and grateful recalling those years.

I later found out that my mother had died from a totally preventable cause. While giving birth to my sister at the construction camp, she had suffered from bleeding complicated by the road dust and lack of medical care. Then she hazarded the six-hour bus ride from Shimla to Dharamsala to visit my father, who had been gravely ill and was at the Tibetan medical clinic there. A few days after her arrival in Dharamsala, my mother passed away. By then my younger brother was already boarding at the Tibetan Children's Village in Dharamsala. With no one to look after my infant sister, she too was left in the care of the Children's Village. I remember visiting the "baby room," the bungalow with a green tin roof and neat rows of cribs, where my sister lived among the other small children, many of them orphans. I waited at the edge of the veranda with some sweets I would give her, and one of the house mothers brought her to me.

Soon after, when my father recovered, he became a monk and joined a monastery.

Thank goodness for my uncle Penpa. My mother's brother was a tall, thin man with high cheekbones and a hint of a limp from a weak knee. Unlike my father, who had worn his hair in the traditional style of two long, red-tasseled braids wrapped around his head, Uncle Penpa kept his hair short and "modern," complemented by a thin mustache. Being an ex-monk, he was literate and had also taught himself enough English to read the signs on the buses and trains. At a time when I felt like an orphan, my uncle Penpa treated me as if I was his own child. Two of his daughters attended my boarding school, and every time Uncle Penpa came to see them, or took them for a holiday to the road construction camp, he included me as well. At the end of these weeklong sojourns, he would give each of us exactly the same amount of pocket money: two Indian rupees. As I grew up and understood more fully the hardships my uncle and my parents experienced in those early days of refugee life in India, I came to appreciate his compassion and kindness even more. They were strangers in a new country, living in makeshift roadside tents, in the relentless rain of the Indian monsoon. Money was scarce, but my uncle shared with me what little he had. Uncle Penpa became one of the most important people in my life and I remained close to him until his death, despite all the changes that took me so far away from his familiar world.

Born to connect

As TV newscasters reminded us in their coverage of the 2013 Boston Marathon bombing, the American educator and television host Fred Rogers once said, "When I was a boy and I would see scary things in the news, my mother would say to me, 'Look for the helpers. You will always find people who are helping.'" We saw them in Boston: onlookers spontaneously rushing into a terrifying scene to help the victims. If we look, we will always find people who are helping, in big ways or small, because it's one of the things we humans were born to do.

My uncle Penpa wasn't a saint. He was a person born, as we all are, with the natural capacity to feel other people's pain and care about their well-being. Extraordinarily compassionate people such as Mother Teresa and the Dalai Lama may seem like they belong to a different species, but they're human too. However, our instinct for compassion is more like our ability to learn a language rather than, say, the color of our eyes. Not everyone will acquire Shakespeare's mastery with words, but we become, through exposure and practice, experts in language in our own way. Mother Teresa and the Dalai Lama got good at compassion because they worked at it. The seed of compassion is present in all of us.

Also, as we will see, small acts of compassion can have a bigger impact than you might expect.

Historically in the West, at least since the Enlightenment, and especially since Darwin's theory of evolution, the dominant view of who we are as a species portrays our basic nature as selfish, with competition as our fundamental drive. Thomas Huxley, often described as Darwin's "bulldog" for his tenacity in propagating Darwin's ideas, used Tennyson's famous phrase "nature red in tooth and claw."[1] Huxley saw human existence as a gladiatorial show, in which "the strongest, the swiftest, and the cunningest live to fight another day."[2] Building on this assumption of our selfish nature, scientists and philosophers have subsequently gone to great lengths to reduce the motive behind every human action to self-interest. If the self-interest underlying a particular behavior had not yet been revealed, the explanation was taken, especially among the scientifically educated, to be incomplete; the notion that any human behavior might be truly selfless was dismissed as a form of naïveté. At best, selfless behavior must be irrational and is possibly detrimental to the person who engages in it. At worst, altruists are hypocrites or deceiving themselves.

I have always found this perspective to be uncharitable toward ourselves, to say the least. In my formative years as a young monk I learned the classical Buddhist view, which understands compassion (and other positive qualities) to be innate, its expression through kindness completely natural. It's a matter of cultivating our better parts, while curbing our more destructive tendencies such as anger, aggression, jealousy, and greed.

Oh, the arguments I used to have about altruism with fellow students at Cambridge! I would cite the example of Mother Teresa and her work for the destitute in the Calcutta slums, and someone would counter, "There must be something in it for her; otherwise she wouldn't be doing it." So, I've been looking my whole career for dissenters to the selfish paradigm. Their ranks are growing in the West, and it will be my pleasure to introduce you to many of them throughout this book. The American philosopher Thomas Nagel, for one, made the case that altruism is not, at least as a concept, incoherent.[3] Psychologist Daniel Batson spent much of his research career demonstrating that genuine selfless human behavior does exist.[4] It seems we humans haven't given ourselves enough credit—and we suffer from the self-fulfilling prophecy of self-ishness.

I am the other

Today, there is a growing recognition even within science that the selfish view of human nature is simplistic.[5] In addition to self-interest, our scientific picture must also embrace the fundamental roles that caring and nurturing instincts play as drivers of human behavior. We recognize cooperation operating in human evolution alongside competition. One important force within this new scientific movement has come from the study of empathy. In disciplines ranging from nonhuman primate studies to child developmental psychology, as well as neuroscience and neuroeconomics (a subset of economics that uses neuroscientific methods to study economic behavior), new research shows that we are motivated by empathy.

What is empathy? It's our natural ability to understand other people's feelings and share in their experience.[6] It thus consists of two key components: an *emotional* response to someone's feelings, and *cognitive* understanding of his or her situation. Our emotional response may take the form of resonance, in which we experience an emotion similar to the other person's, a kind of feeling *with*; or it could be a feeling *for* the other, such as a sense of sorrow for a person's misfortune, without actually feeling what that person is feeling.

The English word *empathy* was coined by the psychologist Edward B. Titchener in 1909 to translate a German mouthful, *einfühlungsvermögen*, which emerged sometime in the nineteenth century. Literally meaning "to be able to feel with," this German term connotes sensitivity to others' feelings. Despite the recent pedigree of the word, people have long recognized the phenomenon. The idea of empathy lies at the heart of the Golden Rule (Do unto others what you would have them do unto you), which underpins the ethical teachings of all major spiritual traditions. In one of the formulations of this rule in the Buddhist sources—"Take your own body as an example/And do not cause harm on others"—the connection with empathy is even more explicit.[7]

The concept of empathy is also present in nonreligious sources. In Jean-Jacques Rousseau's philosophical novel *Emile*, he asks, "How do we let ourselves be moved by pity if not by transporting ourselves outside of ourselves and identifying with the sufferer; by leaving, as it were, our own being to take on its being?"[8] The Scottish philosopher David Hume compares our natural feeling for other people, as we resonate with their pains and pleasures as if they were our own, to the way a violin's strings resonate with the sounds of other strings. Adam Smith, one of the founders of the theory of market economy, thought our imaginative transportation of ourselves into the other is in fact "the source of our fellow-feeling for the misery of others."[9] Charles Darwin himself spoke of our "well-endowed social instincts," and suggested that such instincts "lead an animal to take pleasure in the society of its fellows, to feel a certain amount of sympathy with them, and to perform various services for them."[10]

The Buddhist sources express similar ideas from a different perspective. We read about our natural capacity for empathy arising from our felt sense of connection, or identification, with the other. Some of the early Buddhist texts describe this identification as "clear appreciation" of the other's sentient nature, while other sources characterize it as a "sense of regard for the other" or "valuing the other." In this way, when we empathize we aren't just acknowledging someone else's feelings; we are honoring them.

In the brain, empathy involves several important systems.[11] First and foremost is the limbic system, known especially for its role in processing emotional signals. Second, empathy activates neural networks that are part of the attachment system, which plays a crucial role in the interaction between an infant and an attachment figure such as its mother. Finally, when it arises in response to someone else's suffering, empathy is associated with what scientists call the *pain matrix*, those brain regions associated with our personal experience of pain. Brain imaging indicates that our empathy has deep roots in parts of the brain that are evolutionarily ancient, as well as in newer parts such as the cortical regions that enable us to take on another person's perspective. Findings from neuroscience also indicate how, at least in our human experience of empathy, there is an intimate connection between our perceptions and attitudes on the one hand and our emotions and motivations on the other. So if we change our perception of and attitudes toward someone, we can actually change the way we feel about him or her.

Where the research is taking us

How far back into early childhood do the roots of our caring and kindness go? Two psychologists, Felix Warneken and

Michael Tomasello, examined this question experimentally as a team. They studied whether very young children (fourteen to eighteen months old) exhibit genuine helping behavior.[12] One experiment involved a person hanging a towel on a clothesline and accidentally dropping a clothes peg, which he pretends he can't reach. In another scenario, the experimenter tries to put a stack of magazines inside a cabinet but pretends that he cannot open the cabinet door because his hands are full. In both of these situations, almost all of the children reached out and helped. In subsequent studies, Warneken and Tomasello found that children were willing to help even when doing so involved hardship and interrupting their play.

Interestingly, they also found that rewarding the children was counterproductive. The children who were rewarded for helping were later *less* likely to help than those who had never been rewarded. Studies also show that infants as young as six months demonstrate clear preference for toys that enact helping behavior rather than hindering.[13] If only I'd had this example for my arguments about selflessness at Cambridge.

Personally, I have made similar findings with my own children. When my elder daughter, Khando, was around fifteen months old, my father-in-law was painfully waiting for hip surgery. He needed a stick to walk, and often, to reduce the pain, he would lie flat on his belly on the bed. Khando would spontaneously bring the walking-stick and offer it to him whenever she became aware that her grandfather needed to get up and walk.

What all of these findings suggest is this: Our capacity for empathy, compassion, kindness, and altruistic behavior is inborn, rather than acquired through socialization or cultural exposure. Only later, through socialization, do we begin to differentiate between those who are worthy of our kindness and those who are not. So, to some extent, Rousseau was right when he spoke of society having a corrupting influence on an infant's pure instinct for kindness. As the well-known pioneer in the field of contemplative science Richard Davidson has argued, if our natural capacity for compassion is akin to our capacity for language, then in a person who doesn't encounter compassion (or language) in her formative years, this capacity may unfortunately remain undeveloped and unexpressed.[14]

The benefits of compassion

Empathy is feeling for (or with) other people and understanding their feelings. When we witness another person suffering, in particular, compassion arises from empathy, adding the dimensions of wishing to see the relief of suffering and wanting to do something about it. Compassion is a more empowered state and more than an empathic response to the situation. Kindness is the expression of that compassion through helping, a basic form of altruism. Compassion is what makes it possible for our empathic reaction to manifest in kindness.

Most of us have experienced, at some point in our lives, the power of kindness, or compassion in action. We have felt it as recipients of others' kindness, as I did with my uncle Penpa, and we have been the source of kindness for someone else. Whether it's a simple smile or a kind nod from a colleague when we are eager to be acknowledged, a friend listening patiently as we rant about some frustration, helpful counsel at a critical moment from a teacher who truly cares, a loving hug from a spouse when we feel down, or help from someone during a really hard time, when the rays of kindness touch us we feel relaxed, acknowledged, and valued—in short, we feel affirmed. Too often, though, we forget to be kind or we don't appreciate kindness enough. Helping others is part of the everyday reality of parents, grown-up children looking after their elderly parents, health care workers caring for the sick, and teachers taking care of children everywhere in the world— kindnesses so ubiquitous that we take them for granted. Or we think of kindness as a nice but inessential extra in life, a luxury if anyone can afford the time and energy it takes, when in fact our health, happiness, and our whole world depend on our giving and receiving kindness.

Most of us would say we are compassionate. If you're read- ing this book, probably you would say that compassion is an important part of your identity. That said, most of us have these thoughts about compassion and leave it at that. Unless we work at compassion, unless we practice and change our habits and make it an active force in our lives, it will only be something that happens to us—we get angry when provoked, feel compassion when triggered—an automatic reaction to the pain and needs of our loved ones, or sometimes to strangers in acute distress. If we leave it at that, we fail to tap into the trans- formative power of compassion.

Receiving kindness

Can you think of someone in your own life who has been a figure of kindness for you, the mere recollection of whom fills you with joy and gratitude? It might be a teacher who gently nudged you along at school and helped you to recognize your personal strengths early on. It might be a loyal friend who lets you know she has your back. Or it could be your parents, who provided you with a powerful anchor as you grew up. If no memory of a specific person comes up immediately, leave the question open and sleep on it.

Why is it that the kindness of others, especially when received at a critical point in our lives, has the power to leave such a deep imprint in our minds? The simple answer is that such an act touches us at the deepest level of our humanity—where we are most human—with a powerfully felt need for kindness and connection.

We can all see that we benefit from other people's kindness, but not everyone benefits equally. How much we do benefit appears to be influenced by how compassionate we are ourselves. A team of scientists studied fifty-nine women in the San Francisco Bay Area. Participants filled out a questionnaire that measured their individual level of compassion; they were then randomly divided into two groups. About a week later, the participants came to a laboratory session, where they were asked to do three things: give a speech in the presence of two experimenters, participate in an interview, and work out a maths problem. Each person was given five minutes to think about a speech, while they were hooked up to machines, such as electroencephalographs, that would measure brain waves and certain body functions. For one group, one of the experimenters made positive comments such as "You are doing great," or smiled, nodded in agreement, or made other affirming gestures while the participants engaged in the tasks. For the other group, the experimenters did not offer any positive encouragement.

Strikingly, the participants who scored high on the compassion scale and received supportive signals from an experimenter had lower blood pressure, lower cortisol reactivity, and higher heart rate variability—all proven to be associated with physical health and social well-being—especially during the most stressful of the tasks, giving a speech. Compared to their counterparts in the second group, these same individuals also reported liking the experimenters more. These effects were not observed for those who were in the group that received supportive gestures but scored low on the compassion scale and those who, although scoring high on the compassion scale, did not receive encouragement. In summarizing their findings, the researchers noted that "those who are more compassionate may also be more benefitted by support, particularly during acute stress situations."[15] In other words, to benefit most from others' kindness we need to be ready with kindness of our own.

The helper's high

It goes both ways. When we do something kind for another person out of compassion, we feel good ourselves, because kindness affirms something fundamental to our human condition—our need for and appreciation of connection with fellow humans. Compassion and kindness also free us from the strangling confines of self-involvement and let us feel part of something larger. If we normally plod along in our daily existence wearing blinkers of self-focused worry and rumination, compassion takes the blinkers off and puts our lives in perspective with the world.

It's no surprise, then, that scientists have identified positive effects of compassion in the brain. When we help someone with genuine concern for her well-being, levels of endorphins, which are associated with euphoric feeling, surge in the brain, a phenomenon referred to as the helper's high. In studies in which participants were asked to consciously extend compassion to another person, the reward centers of the compassionate brain were activated—the same brain system that lights up when we think of chocolate or another treat. So, in a sense, my fellow Cambridge students were right: Even for Mother Teresa, there was something in it for her, though not in the selfish sense they assumed. The fulfillment Mother Teresa derived from her selfless service was a by-product, not the goal. Her primary motive was to bring help and solace to the destitute. This is the catch—a happy catch—to compassion: The more we are in it for other people, the more we get out of it ourselves.

Other studies have shown that children report increased happiness when they have been encouraged to act kindly,[16] and that engaging in acts of kindness leads to an increase in peer acceptance—a big deal for teenagers. Peer acceptance is also a key to reducing bullying at school.

It's a paradox of happiness itself that we are happier when we are less concerned with our own happiness. From being inspired to being in love, our deepest experiences of happiness come from transcending our narrow selves. The birth of my first daughter comes to mind. Even on a mundane level, we know we tend to forget ourselves when we're having a good time. (And vice versa: Self-consciousness is such a barrier to happiness that people go to great, sometimes self-destructive lengths to escape it, for example with alcohol or other intoxicants.)

When we feel compassionate toward someone, we see the whole world colored in a positive light. On the surface, this is counterintuitive. Common sense suggests that compassion's focus on suffering would make the world look bleak and us feel pessimistic. However, a study I was involved in at Stanford's psychology lab suggests the opposite.[17] We showed undergraduates images of people's faces and asked them to consciously extend compassion to some of these. After a break, the participants viewed images of modern art and rated them. But before each art slide, one of the face images flashed up for a fraction of a second, too quickly to consciously recognize. The students rated the art far more positively if it followed the faces to which they had earlier extended compassion. This link—feeling compassion and perceiving the world in a more positive light—may explain why compassionate individuals generally tend to be more optimistic as well.

More compassion, more purpose

For me, the most compelling thing about compassion and kindness is how they bring purpose to our life. There is nothing like the feeling of being useful. Whether at home or at work, when we can make a difference helping others we feel energized and oriented, more effective and in control. Having a purpose in life turns out to be one of the crucial factors of personal happiness, and it even affects our longevity. A comprehensive study on the effects of a three-month meditation program that included compassion practice found especially interesting effects on the participants' telomerase, an enzyme that repairs our telomeres.[18] Telomeres are the tail-like ends of DNA molecules, which get shortened over time through the process of replication and are associated with aging. Remarkably, in participants with high scores for having a sense of purpose in life the study found an increase of telomerase, suggesting a slowing of the aging process. Several large-scale studies of elderly populations have also shown how volunteering slows aging (again, this benefit was observed only when the voluntary work was done with the sincere wish to help others).

More compassion, less stress

The Dalai Lama often says that being more compassionate can make us feel less stressed. This too might seem incredible, since compassion depends on acknowledging the unpleasant facts of our own and others' vulnerability and suffering, but science agrees. The trick, as with happiness, seems to be the release from the stress of judging and worrying about ourselves. With a compassionate shift of focus from our own narrow self-agenda (and the heaviness that tends to go with it) to others, we feel lighter. The same stressors may exist in our lives, but we feel less stressed out by them. For what makes our normal response to stress so stressful is how it weighs us down and how we fear it will overwhelm us. Compassion, on the other hand, lightens us up. We feel our individual burden lift a little. We see it in perspective. We realize we're not carrying it alone.

Another way compassion helps buffer stress is through the

understanding and tolerance that tends to go with it. We feel less annoyed and offended by others when we can feel compassion for them instead. With greater self-compassion, in particular, we can be gentler and more patient with our own perceived failings. It turns out that judging ourselves harshly, feeling ashamed, and trying to hide our imperfections is really stressful! With the self-honesty, self-acceptance, and self-transparency of self-compassion, we have nothing to hide; and with nothing to hide, we have less to be afraid of.

A study of Harvard undergraduates preparing for the GRE (Graduate Record Examinations) required for admissions into postgraduate programs in most American universities showed how even a simple intervention using "reappraisal"—understanding stress-related symptoms in positive terms (for example, that a raised heart rate predicted better, not worse, performance)—changed how the students responded to the stress associated with taking the exam.[19] Those who had reappraised the situation were also able to return to their baseline more quickly, once the stressful event had passed. (As it happened, they also scored better on the test.) In fact, lack of self-compassion is so stressful and so endemic in the modern world that we'll spend the whole next chapter on it.

Finally, as we have seen, being disposed toward compassion lets us benefit more from social support, another proven cushion against the long-term negative impacts of stress. The warm feeling we get from our own compassion has been found to help release the hormone oxytocin—the same hormone released by lactating mothers—which is associated with reduced levels of inflammation in the cardiovascular system, an important factor that plays a role in heart disease. As we shall see later, studies have also shown how cultivating concern for the well-being of others helps strengthen the tone of our vagus nerve. This nerve, the longest cranial nerve, regulates our heart rate, modulates inflammation levels within the body, and is a marker of our overall state of health.

The cure for loneliness

Clearly, compassion contributes to better relationships. Kindness acts like glue that keeps our connections with our loved ones strong and protects us against the fissures or breaks that disagreements and emotional distance may cause. Researchers have found that social connection strengthens our immune system. So kindness, as a key factor in forming and maintaining social connection, helps keep our immune system healthy. In romantic relationships, being kind makes us more attractive. Looking back, I realize that one of the things that attracted me to my wife was her kindness, and her big heart and beautiful smile that go with it.

It follows that compassion fights loneliness, one of the most painful forms of suffering. By helping us connect with others, compassion dissolves the barriers that make us feel isolated. The importance of this side effect cannot be overstated. A recent study from the University of Chicago tracked more than two thousand people over the age of fifty for a period of six years and found that extreme loneliness is twice as likely to cause death among the elderly as obesity or high blood pressure. Those who had reported being lonely had a 14 percent greater risk of dying.[20] Some studies suggest that extreme loneliness is more dangerous than cigarette smoking.

Scientists speak of loneliness as a kind of pain on our "social body," and it needs to be remedied if we are to live a healthy life. All the lonely people are like fish swimming at the edge of a school, exposed to the threat of predators. The constant vigilance required to live with such threat has been associated with much higher cortisol levels in the morning—fight or flight before the day has even begun. Prolonged loneliness, over time, damages our hormonal balance and nervous system.

Sadly, loneliness is becoming an epidemic. This will surely have major implications, in terms of both individual suffering and public health care costs. A sociological study found that around 25 percent of Americans report that they have no one to confide in.[21] A separate 2012 British study revealed more than one-fifth of the participants felt lonely most of the time, out of which a quarter reported becoming even lonelier during the five-year study period.[22]

No doubt there is a link between today's widespread loneliness and contemporary culture's emphasis on autonomy and an individualistic lifestyle, both of which tend to undermine social connectedness. Can the rise of social networking opportunities such as Facebook reverse this cultural trend toward greater loneliness? The research so far is inconclusive; it's too early to say, but I doubt it. If anything, with declining human-to-human interaction, chances are our younger generation might experience loneliness even more acutely.

I witnessed the Dalai Lama hug a total stranger once. His Holiness was participating in a seminar on Buddhism and Psychotherapy in Newport Beach, California, and I was his interpreter. One afternoon, among the small group of people waiting outside the home where the Dalai Lama was staying, a visibly disturbed man shouted out to him. His Holiness walked toward him and patiently listened to the man rant about the pointlessness of living. The Dalai Lama then urged the man to think about the good things in his life, and the importance of his presence in the lives of his loved ones, as well as the good things he could do with his life by helping others. Nothing worked. So, finally, His Holiness stopped talking and gave the man a huge bear hug. The man sobbed loudly, then became calm and relaxed.

Findings from numerous studies show, not too surprisingly, that real-life social connectedness is the cure for loneliness. Opening our heart to others, caring for others, and allowing our heart to be touched by others' kindness—living our life in ways that express our compassionate core—creates strong social connections. We are born to connect. Our longing for connection, not just with our fellow humans but with animals, is so deep that it determines our experience of happiness.

Kindness is contagious

One of the most exciting recent findings from science in this domain, especially considering the loneliness epidemic, is that kindness catches on. Other people's kindness makes us kinder. Not only do we feel good when we see someone help another person; we are moved to help someone ourselves. Some researchers have dubbed this phenomenon "moral elevation," drawing on Thomas Jefferson's observation of how we become altruistically inspired when we see or think about acts of charity.[23] Imagine a ripple effect of kindness. Starting from each of us, the effects of kindness spread outward, with each person affected creating another circle of effects and so on, eventually resulting in multiple overlapping circles ...

Next time when you observe someone being kind—showing concern to another person or helping someone in difficulty—see if you can notice how you instinctively react. Without any conscious thought, do your eyes light up? Does your heart feel lifted? Does your mouth shape itself into a gentle smile?

Three scientists—from Cambridge University, Plymouth University, and the University of California, Los Angeles—demonstrated compassion's contagious nature with an ingenious experiment.[24] Their study compared university students randomly assigned into two groups. One group viewed TV clips of comedy or nature programs, while the second group was exposed to uplifting scenes (from *The Oprah Winfrey Show*) that involved people helping others. Told that the experiment would test memory, the participants were asked to complete a computer task pertaining to what they had seen. As the task was supposed to begin, the experimenter pretended to have trouble opening the computer file. Failing several attempts, the experimenter then told the participant that he or she was free to go and would receive the promised course credits anyway. As the student rose to leave, the experimenter asked, seemingly as an afterthought, whether the student was willing to fill out another questionnaire to aid the experimenter's research on a separate project. The questionnaire was designed to be boring and tedious, and there would be no compensation.

The results were striking. The participants who had watched acts of kindness were more likely to help the experimenter with the unpaid study. Of those who agreed to help, participants in the Oprah group spent twice as much time doing so. Witnessing kindness makes us feel compassionate, and compassion predicts helping behavior.

Fortunately, opportunities for kindness are abundant in everyday life. We can kiss our loved ones good-bye in the morning, give our seat on the bus to a pregnant woman, let a driver in a rush pass us on the road, or offer a colleague a caring ear; we can volunteer our time; we can donate a part of our income to help others. Most of us have plenty of opportunities for kindness every day, if we think about it. And if we're not in the habit of thinking about it, we can learn—Part II of this book will show you how.

Around the world, people have organized to promote kindness. In the "pay it forward" movement, instead of repaying a good deed back to the person who did it, people spread the kindness by doing something for somebody else. In many schools, kindness is now part of the curriculum. In Britain, a campaign to promote a million "random acts of kindness" was launched on the BBC in 2008, and today "random acts of kindness" is a common phrase. Imagine if compassion were no longer a *secret* of happiness, but a celebrated value, an organizing principle of society, and a driving force of change?

Hanging in there with patience

Usually our loved ones are our primary benefactors of kindness, our greatest source of happiness. And for the very same reason, they can also be the greatest cause of our hurt feelings. Feeling compassion for a loved one might come naturally now and again. But to sustain kindness on an ongoing basis, especially in the face of adversity, requires patience and dedication. Often the nitty-gritty of everyday interactions in the charged atmosphere of family relations makes it hard to retain the composure so essential for compassion to manifest. When this happens, we need to be kind and forgiving of ourselves. (We will learn about the importance of self-compassion in the next chapter, and techniques for maintaining composure in Part II.)

We also need to remind ourselves of a basic truth about close relationships: Sharp and painful exchanges occur because we care for each other and feel safe enough to let down our guard. As long as both sides keep sight of this truth, kindness will remain at the core of the relationship.

In my own life, one of the most challenging relationships I have had was with my father. From ages eleven to twenty, I was a member of the same small monastery as my father, Dzongkar Choede, named after the one in the town of Dzongkar in Western Tibet, where I was born. My father had strong emotional ties to this monastery and its long history. My trouble began after I completed the monastic training—mainly memorization of liturgical texts and chanting—when I began taking interest in other things, such as learning English and reading texts not connected with the monastery's needs. I was intellectually restless and increasingly uncomfortable with our everyday ritual, especially chanting from texts without knowing their meaning.

Once he'd accepted my decision to join the monastery in the

first place, my father's aspiration for me was straightforward: He saw me eventually becoming the chant master, the ritual master, and the abbot of that small monastery. I had other ideas, and being a permanent member of that community wasn't one of them. Barely literate, my father never understood my intellectual curiosity and took it as a form of teenage defiance that would pass. He accused me of being selfish and ungrateful for the hardship he and my mother had endured for us. Pushing myself away from the community, he believed, would lead to loss of respect and misery for me. On my part too, I began to shut him out, making our relationship even more strained and alienated.

I left Dzongkar Choede to join an academic monastery in another part of southern India, and so opened a new chapter in my life. Although we kept in close touch with each other, I could see that I had become a source of disappointment and embarrassment for my father. He believed I had betrayed the community—loyalty is a prized virtue for Tibetans, as it is in many Asian cultures.

Everything changed in 1985, when I became an English translator to His Holiness the Dalai Lama. Ever since, in my father's eyes, I could do nothing wrong. He acknowledged that he had failed to understand me, and that he never knew that all the "wild things" I had done could have such beneficial applications.

In the last decade of my father's life, he suffered from Parkinson's. The strong dopamine-inducing medication that helped him with mobility made him quite unhappy, exacerbating his anxious personality and causing frequent episodes of paranoia and psychosis, which somehow also heightened his fear of death. I was fortunate to be able to spend time helping him come to terms with his fears, mainly through Buddhist spiritual teachings and meditations. He died in peace, happy knowing that he had led a good life and that all three of his children—my brother, my sister, and I—are happy and have families of our own. I have to admit that there were times I could have given up and said to hell with our relationship. Through compassion—for him and for myself—I stuck with it.

What makes us engage in acts of kindness toward others? What is the engine that drives such acts? And what sustains them so that we continue to find them worthy of our attention and effort?

Clearly, it is the caring, compassionate part of our nature that is the force. While it makes us vulnerable in the sense of needing other people's care and kindness, it also endows us with the ability to connect with others—their needs, their pain, and their joys. It is this caring instinct that helps us connect with others at the most basic level. In fact, when we feel kind and compassionate toward someone, when we are connected with another's pains and needs, we feel most alive as human beings. We feel energized; even our physical heart reacts with greater force, priming our body so that it is ready to act. In the midst of compassion, in a sense, we are stripped of all the categories and labels that we have constructed about ourselves to individuate us from others, and our humanity is revealed. It is at this basic level that we connect with the person in front of us. In that moment, what matters is that this person is just another human being—just like us—who aspires to happiness and who instinctively avoids suffering. Nothing else matters: not race, not religion, not cultural affiliation, and not gender. To act from this place in response to the other person's need is to act out of true kindness.

2

The Key to Self-Acceptance

Having Compassion for Yourself

The deepest principle in human nature is the craving to be appreciated.

—William James (1842–1910)

The root of wisdom lies in observing our own mind.

—Gönpawa (11th century)

We gravitate toward other people's kindness, and, when we let ourselves, we can instinctively respond to others' needs with compassion. This intertwining susceptibility of self and others lies at the heart of our humanness. Given this reality, we might assume that self-compassion—being caring and kind toward ourselves—must be as natural as breathing, something we can all do without learning it or even thinking about it. Actually, the situation turns out to be more complicated, especially in today's highly competitive society.

Contemporary culture makes it hard for many of us to have

compassion for ourselves. And yet, according to a steady stream of evidence emerging from scientific studies, so much seems to hang on our ability to do just that. From anxiety disorders to burnout at work, from relationship troubles to motivation and couch-potato problems, our self-compassion—or lack thereof—makes a big difference. When we lack self-compassion, we are less self-accepting, less self-tolerant, and less kind to ourselves. These deficiencies manifest in many unhelpful ways in our own lives and in our interactions with others, especially the people we love. Self-compassion is every bit as critical to our happiness as our compassion for others, if not more, yet for many people it feels as alien and uncomfortable as walking on their hands. If we're not used to it, it will take some practice.

What self-compassion is not

This chapter is about what self-compassion is, and why it is good. But there's so much misunderstanding about it that I would like to clarify a few things first.

It's still true that we're happier when we're less self-focused and more oriented toward the world, but self-compassion is totally different from narcissistic self-absorption. Truly self-compassionate people take care of themselves while being attentive to the feelings and needs of those around them. In fact, the mental and physical health that comes from being kind to ourselves enables us to take *better* care of other people. When we are self-centered, on the other hand, we are so caught up in our own world that we don't have room for anyone else.

Self-compassion should not be confused with self-pity, either. In self-pity, we get caught up in our own problems and, feeling sorry for ourselves, we become oblivious to the world around us. Self-pity is a form of self-absorption, whereas self-compassion allows us to see our difficulties within the larger context of shared human experience. Because of its narrow, zoom-lens focus, self-pity tends to blow up our situation so that even a small problem appears overwhelming and unbearable. In contrast, self-compassion affords a sense of proportion that helps us deal with our predicaments and suffering in more constructive ways.

Self-compassion is not self-gratification. The most compassionate thing we can do for ourselves may be to *not* eat the whole bag of donuts, or to *not* confuse wanting with needing and buy something we don't need. Self-compassion is not an impulse to "treat ourselves," though sometimes, mindfully and upon reflection, we may decide to have a treat. Equally important: Self-compassion is not beating ourselves up for eating the donuts, or buying the thing, or having the treat.

Finally, self-compassion is not the same as self-esteem. With self-compassion, we relate to ourselves, especially our struggles and failures, with understanding, kindness, and acceptance. Self-compassion is a gentle, caring, clear-seeing yet nonjudgmental orientation of our heart and mind toward our own suffering and needs. Self-esteem, on the other hand, is self-regard based on self-evaluation. While self-compassion may contribute to increased self-esteem, it does not depend on it.

In contemporary culture, especially in North America, self-esteem has become the Holy Grail of child development and mental health. In the United States, schools have programs aimed at boosting self-esteem. Parents get the message that it's never too early to start worrying about their children's self-esteem. Certainly, there is nothing wrong with self-esteem per se. But it is too often tied to criteria of achievement, which leads people, including children, to believe that they are worthy of esteem (from themselves and others) only to the degree that they "succeed." And self-esteem is twisted by our competitive culture, so that many people understand their worth only in comparison with other people.

As parents, sometimes my wife and I are tempted to play this game, boosting our daughters' self-esteem through their accomplishments in their studies or sports or music. But, as someone who grew up in a very different culture, I worry about the implications of such a conditional definition of self-worth. Growing up, I never believed that my value as a person was contingent on how good I was at this or that. Even as a child, I felt like a complete person, acknowledged in my own right as an individual. This may have to do with the traditional Buddhist idea that each one of us brings something unique, drawn from our past karma (everything that happened before and during our lifetime that created the circumstances we find ourselves in) into the rich network of human relationships.

Some scientists have raised similar concerns. Researchers have discovered that achievement-dependent self-esteem makes us vulnerable to feelings of inadequacy and failure when things don't unfold as expected. Some researchers offer evidence that the pursuit of self-esteem may hinder learning, specifically learning from our mistakes. When our purpose in doing something is the validation we anticipate from positive results—running for the sake of winning and feeling like a winner, say, instead of running because it's good for us, it helps us manage our depression, and it's a nice day outside—we are not well equipped to deal with negative results. Then when failure and disappointment confront us, as inevitably they will, we feel personally threatened by them. Either we pretend that everything is fine (denial), or we go to the other extreme and judge ourselves harshly.[1]

The question for my wife and me was: Is it possible to have the benefits associated with high self-esteem—confidence and optimism, for example—without the negative side effects of its pursuit? Can self-esteem and self-compassion be compatible? Yes, if self-esteem is achieved as a by-product, rather than pursued directly for its own sake. The active ingredient we want from self-esteem is *self-liking*, not self-perfecting, self-aggrandizing, or self-promoting. Self-liking implies an easygoing peace with ourselves. Crucially, the self-liking that comes from self-compassion is devoid of hubris. Self-compassion combines self-worth and genuine humility.

Tibetans encapsulate the problems with perfectionistic self-esteem in the memorable saying "Envy toward the above, competitiveness toward the equal, and contempt toward the lower." These, they say, often lie at the root of our dissatisfaction and unhappiness.

In cultivating self-compassion, we don't evaluate ourselves according to our worldly successes, and we don't compare ourselves with others. Instead, we acknowledge our shortcomings and failings with patience, understanding, and kindness. We view our problems within the larger context of our shared human condition. So, self-compassion, unlike self-esteem, lets us feel more connected with other people, and more positively disposed toward them. Finally, self-compassion lets us be honest with ourselves. With its attitude of acceptance, self-compassion promotes a realistic understanding of our situation. If the results of preliminary studies are any indication, our capacity for self-compassion might also be quite flexible and amenable to change.

There was a woman in her forties who did our compassion training course at Stanford. She had suffered a stroke that left her partially paralyzed on one side of her body. Until she took the course, she felt unable to bathe the affected side of her body because she couldn't bring herself to touch it. She required assistance to wash herself. By extending compassion and kindness toward that side of her body, she overcame her aversion and could bathe her whole body again. She also reported a powerful effect on her quality of life and sense of well-being as a result of this change.[2]

To the naive eye of someone who grew up in a poorer part of the world, at first glance, people in the West seem more confident, more efficient, and better able to take care of themselves and enjoy life. Many people in this individualistic society have only themselves to look after, or at most a few others in their immediate family. Families are small, and aging parents live separately, often in retirement homes. Leisure is highly valued in this culture. Holidays are an established custom, much as in other places and times, people went on religious pilgrimages. In short, we seem dedicated to self-care, contentment, and celebrating life. But all is not as it seems.

We can see signs of people's lack of self-compassion—from disliking to loathing to hatred—just about everywhere we look, in countless forms. To name a few: People stay in dysfunctional or abusive relationships because they blame themselves for what's not working and don't believe they deserve better. People are uncomfortable in their bodies, don't like what they see in the mirror, and starve themselves, stuff themselves, or hurt themselves to distract themselves from their real pain. People don't care about themselves, or tell themselves they don't, because as soon as they do they feel overwhelmed. And people don't take care of themselves, neglecting their basic needs for sleep, nutrition, and exercise, and drive themselves harder and harder at work because they don't know how else to find validation as human beings. People lash out or shut down when they are criticized, because they are all too ready to believe anything bad about themselves, but at the same time they can't stand to hear anything bad about themselves because they lack a sense of self-worth to balance it. People feel like frauds, *especially* when things are going well. They live in fear that one day they'll be exposed, because they don't actually believe they deserve anything good. People feel anxious and depressed and desperate and they don't know what to do—and they blame and berate themselves for this too.

I was brought up to believe that self-caring—an expression of self-compassion—is an instinct that not just humans but all sentient beings share. The traditional Buddhist compassion meditations, for example, operate from the premise that we have the instinct to be kind to ourselves, and the technique involves extending this natural feeling toward others in expanding circles of concern: from ourselves to our loved ones to strangers to "difficult" people (politicians we disagree with, teenagers we're having trouble communicating with, and so on) and eventually to everybody and every being everywhere. Traditionally, we understand self-compassion as the basis from which we learn to become more compassionate and caring toward others.

I saw this traditional Buddhist assumption of self-compassion come face-to-face with contemporary experience in 1989 at the Newport Beach conference on Buddhism and psychotherapy, where the Dalai Lama was fully exposed to the concept of self-hatred for the first time. In one of the panel discussions, therapists spoke of entrenched self-hatred at the heart of many of their patients' problems.[3] The Dalai Lama was baffled when they asked how Buddhist techniques might help with this in therapy. Initially, His Holiness questioned the very coherence of the concept—if self-preservation, self-care, and self-love are fundamental instincts of every sentient creature, as Buddhist psychology assumes, how could we hate our very being? How could we become so unhinged and alienated from our own nature? Self-hatred is not a simple matter of not liking how you look or not being satisfied with what you have accomplished in life, or even a lack of self-esteem. Self-hatred seemed to suggest, to the Dalai Lama, something much more problematic at the core of our self-relation. The panelists had to work hard to convince His Holiness that not only is the concept coherent, it is a psychological reality, and not uncommon in the West.

It's not that the Buddhist assumptions are wrong. In fact, the Dalai Lama now understands that self-hatred is rooted in the very same self-caring instinct. Hatred is a form of caring (we don't hate if we don't care). Self-hatred comes from caring a lot but being unable to accept or forgive our imperfect selves. With self-compassion training, we learn to reconnect with the part of us that still cares, purely, tenderly, and vulnerably. It never stopped; it's just been hidden behind the layers of armor we put on when we feel like we're under attack.

Having now lived in the West for more than two decades, I have seen the problem of a lack of self-compassion up close in many forms. Even so, I sometimes underestimate its reach in people's everyday lives. When I first developed compassion cultivation training at Stanford, I retained the traditional Buddhist stages progressing from self-compassion to compassion for others in an ever-expanding circle. But when we tested the program on undergraduate students, it became clear that self-compassion, meant to be a launching pad, was for this population a stumbling block. Many reported feeling uncomfortable when they thought about their own needs. Some had aversive reactions to self-compassionate meditation phrases such as "May I be happy; may I find peace and joy." I realized we needed to start somewhere else or we'd be stuck there, and I changed the order of the steps in the course.

I spoke about this problem of self-compassion in the West with Kristin Neff, a psychologist who has been instrumental in bringing a systematic scientific approach to the topic. As part of her seminal work on the psychology of self-compassion, Neff has developed a questionnaire aimed at measuring what she sees as the three main components of self-compassion: self-kindness, common humanity, and mindfulness.[4] She explains self-kindness as relating to our shortcomings and difficulties with kindness, understanding, and acceptance rather than negative judgment. Common humanity, in her scale, is how we perceive our problems and suffering within the context of shared human experience. And mindfulness is the ability to hold painful experiences in awareness, instead of over-identifying with them through obsessive thinking or desperately trying to fix them.

For example, would you agree or disagree with the following statements? How strongly? Very strongly, somewhat, or not at all?

- I try to be understanding and patient toward those aspects of my personality I don't like. (Self-kindness)

- When I'm going through a very hard time, I give myself the caring and tenderness I need. (Self-kindness)

- When I feel inadequate in some way, I try to remind myself that feelings of inadequacy are shared by most people. (Common humanity)

- When things are going badly for me, I see the difficulties as part of life that everyone goes through. (Common humanity)

- When I'm feeling down I try to approach my feelings with curiosity and openness. (Mindfulness)

- When I fail at something important to me I try to keep things in perspective. (Mindfulness)

(Kristin Neff offers a free self-compassion test online at http://www.centerformsc.org/self-compassion_test.)

Neff assures me that the self-compassion shortage is really not about East versus West. Her self-compassion scale has now been applied across many countries, both in the West and in the East, and the problem appears to be as widespread in many Asian countries as it is in the United States, Canada, and Europe. A study comparing the United States, Taiwan, and Thailand revealed Thailand's score for self-compassion to be highest, with the United States coming a distant second and Taiwan last among the three.[5] Neff and her colleagues attribute the Thais' higher score to their Buddhist culture. I suspect that it may also be linked to the greater sense of connection individual Thais feel within their shared cultural heritage. In any case, the problem appears to have more to do with modernity and contemporary culture than the Judeo-Christian heritage of the West versus the Asian cultural heritage of the East.

The high cost of low self-compassion

There is no doubt that contemporary culture tends to promote individual autonomy and respect for the basic rights of the individual, and for many good and well-known reasons. But this comes at a psychological cost. As we cut the ties of interdependency and move further away from a communal experience of life, this places the burden of making sense of our existence upon the shoulders of each one of us separately. Since each of us now has to create his or her own meaning, we become obsessed with what we accomplish, to the point where we define our personal identity and evaluate our self-worth in terms of our work—hence the question "What do you do?" which has come to mean so much more than "What do you do for a living?"

My wife teases me for being a workaholic compared with most Tibetans. Perhaps some performance orientation is unavoidable in any competitive environment, but too often we take it to regrettable extremes. I read a news story with horror about how in South Korea there were after-school tutorial centers that would remain open way past midnight. Concerned about the psychological health of these students, government agencies felt the need to enforce a curfew, forbidding these after-school centers to remain open after ten p.m.[6] Performance obsession can lead to insensitivity, impatience, and even arrogance toward other people, especially when we perceive them to be not up to our standard.

Lack of self-compassion manifests in a harsh and judgmental relationship with ourselves. Many people believe that unless they are critical and demanding of themselves, they will be failures, unworthy of recognition and undeserving of love. If we listen, is there a voice in our head relentlessly doubting, in one way or another? "Do I really deserve to be happy?" "Why should good things happen to me?" "Am I worthy of being loved?" Or perhaps the voice doesn't ask; it just tells us we're not worthy. When something good does happen, we may feel deep down that we don't deserve it. We worry that we might somehow be forced to pay for it afterward. We're terrified of letting go even a little, because we think we'll lose control of our lives—something bad might happen, and we'll blame ourselves. We're afraid that if we were to be gentle and kind with ourselves, to relax our grip, we might not accomplish anything at all. So we keep cracking our internal whip. It's exhausting, struggling against the voice of our judgmental selves all the time just to carry on.

A study conducted on undergraduates at Duke and Wake Forest universities found striking connections between an individual's self-compassion and how he or she responds to adverse experiences.[7] Those who scored low on self-compassion were more likely to think at the end of a bad day, "I'm a loser," or "My life is really screwed up." When asked to recall failures they may have had in academic, athletic, or social domains, those with lower self-compassion were more likely to think, "I am such a loser," "I wish I could die," and so on. They were also more likely to get upset or feel defensive when receiving objective feedback from a peer.

To make matters worse, when study participants were asked to give a short speech (a standard lab test to induce stress), those in the audience responded less positively to the speakers with lower self-compassion. We can see how this could be a vicious cycle: The audience picks up on the energy of low self-compassion, and their negative response makes the speaker feel more uncomfortable, and so on.

As parents, my wife and I watch our daughters for two common forms of self-harshness. One is a generalizing tendency in the face of adverse experience: We turn failure and disappointment in a specific situation into a universal characteristic. For example, when our relationship with a friend breaks down, we speed off with thoughts like, "Something is wrong with me," "I'm never going to make friends again," and so on. When we see our daughters react along these lines, we try to help them to stay with the particulars of the incident. Staying with the concrete facts helps keep the problem more manageable. We also try to notice if they personalize adverse experience with categorical negative judgments such as "I'm stupid," "I'm a loser," "I'm a failure," and so on, when the objective truth is more like "I had trouble with that assignment," or "I felt embarrassed." We discourage them from using the harsher, self-damning kinds of phrases even casually. (Even after so many years of living in the West, I find them quite jarring.) Whether or not you're a parent, one way to think about self-compassion is as being a good parent to yourself.

Some say that without self-compassion, we can't be compassionate toward others. I disagree. Compassion for others, especially for those in need, is a natural human instinct. We also see compassionate and altruistic people who are, at the same time, harsh and intolerant when it comes to themselves, or people who are good friends to others whom they would never consider treating as meanly as they treat themselves. It's all too possible for caregivers, such as parents, to turn themselves inside out with love and concern for others while neglecting their need for self-compassion. Or someone who works for social justice may be heroic in his job helping others, but personally angry, bitter, impatient—and unbearable to his family at home. Self-neglect can be a form of escapism, when sorting out other people is easier than sorting out ourselves. In the long run, however, this will prove unhealthy, even pathological (psychologists use the term *pathological altruism*[8]), if the caregiver invests his identity and purpose in what the person he's caring for achieves in life, and the relationship becomes suffocating as a result. Neglecting our own needs can lead to emotional burnout over time, leaving us depleted and exhausted. It's a common problem for those in the frontline of health care and social work, and anyone with an empathetic disposition and strong sense of social justice. Unchecked, this emotional burnout can cause people to end up feeling resentful and used—even abused—by the people they care for. When this happens, it's truly sad.

The benefits of self-compassion

Renewing our resources

I like to think of cultivating self-compassion as replenishing a wellspring of kindness and compassion that lies within. To use a more contemporary metaphor, it's like recharging our inner battery so that we have more kindness and compassion to draw from for others. With greater self-compassion we protect ourselves against burnout, pessimism, and despair as we face the sometimes enormous challenges of life.

Setting realistic goals

When we are more concerned with our true needs and well-being than with what society or certain people think or expect from us, we can set goals that are both more personally meaningful and more doable. Plus, the more a goal means to us, the more committed and motivated we tend to feel about it.

Learning from our experience

With more self-compassion we are less likely to get stuck in self-judgment and defeatism when we experience setbacks along the way. Self-compassion emphasizes how we relate to inevitable disappointments and failures, so it frees us from the impossible task of trying to construct a disappointment- and failure-free life. Self-compassion is encouraging—and when we are less afraid of our mistakes, we can more readily look them in the eye, learn what we can from them, and move on with our greater goals in mind. Self-compassion makes us more resilient in the face of challenges. And the understanding, acceptance, and sense of proportion as we relate to the world that self-compassion entails is a kind of wisdom in itself.

Feeling less alone

As Kristin Neff's scale reflects, part of self-compassion is to understand our problems and predicaments within the larger context of the human condition. Instead of asking, "Why me?" we see, "I am not alone."

"Be kind, and be happy"

In 1981, when I was twenty-two years old, a softening in Chinese policy inside Tibet made it possible for my maternal grandmother to come to Katmandu, Nepal, along with two of my aunts and an uncle. My grandmother was already in her late eighties then. Unaware that my mother had been dead for many years, she sent a message asking my mother and my uncle Penpa—the two of her children who had escaped to India in 1959—to meet her and her family in Katmandu. When my uncle suggested that I accompany him as the eldest of my mother's three children, I said no.

The last thing I wanted to do was to interrupt my studies at the monastery and travel all the way from South India to Katmandu to meet someone I had never even seen before. A few days after my uncle left, I received a stern telegram from my monastery teacher, Zemey Rinpoche, who also happened to be visiting Nepal at the time. (In India in those days, only the rich could afford to telephone.) Rinpoche's telegram read something like this: *Come immediately STOP Don't be foolish STOP If you don't see grandma this time, you will regret all life STOP Confirm departure STOP.* Needless to say, I did end up going, but only grudgingly at first.

Meeting my grandmother brought home powerfully how my initial refusal came from a part of me that was least kind. It came from a place of excessive self-preoccupation, where I was being driven by an obsession with "efficiency"—in this case my studies at the monastery—that closed me to other possibilities of life's blessings. And there was arrogance in it. Clearly, I had not thought about what the reunion could mean to my grandmother, who would be learning of the death of her own daughter, my mother.

As it turned out, this trip to Katmandu was one of the most memorable experiences of my life. The long journey from South India to Katmandu—three days by train to the last major town before the Nepalese border and then a daylong bus ride through some of the most impressive landscapes of the Himalayan region—offered one of the most reflective times I experienced as a young man.

My grandmother, *Mo mo la*, as we say in Tibetan, had a typical Tibetan nomadic woman's face with a natural smile that lit up effortlessly. Judging by her face, she could have been anywhere from sixty to ninety years old. The lines on her fore-head were deep and the skin of her face toughened by years of exposure to high-altitude sun. She wore the traditional Tibetan *chupa* with a colorful checkered apron, as well as two golden earrings studded with flat polished turquoise. Just like my mother, she wore her hair in two braids, red and turquoise-colored tassels at each end, wrapped around her head. She had a square patch of medical tape stuck to each temple, suppos-edly to prevent migraines. But the most striking thing about her was her eyes.

There was a commotion as I walked into the room where my grandmother and her family were gathered. Everybody, includ-ing my elderly grandmother, rushed to hug me, and they were practically wailing. Although I had never met them before, I too felt the collective pain of long separation and the grief over my mother's absence. There, in that room, were all my grand-mother's children, except for one, my mother. Once things calmed down, there was a long pause of silence, which was strangely peaceful and comforting.

It was a privilege to spend a week in my grandmother's gentle, compassionate presence, seeing her interact with my aunts and uncles. She had a natural sense of ease with herself, a genuine and free air about her. Perhaps it was age and wisdom, but I felt that this level of serenity had to come from something deeper, in the contrast between the kind of life she led and the life I was living. Despite us both being Tibetans, our two lives were totally different. She was an uneducated, illiterate woman, while I was a student of Buddhist thought, trained in the famed Tibetan debating tradition, and, through my command of English, I had access to the outside world. Yet my grandmother felt sorry for me; I could see it in her eyes. I was then a restless, ambitious monk, rarely living in the present, always glancing into the future. Sensing my grandmother's compassion, seeing the profound beauty of a person so comfortable in her skin that she was completely at ease with herself and open to the people around her, right then and there, I started to wonder what I'd lost in the course of becoming educated and obsessed with performance, efficiency, and progress. I would continue to wonder about this.

When we said good-bye, we hugged and she touched my forehead with hers in the traditional Tibetan gesture. Holding my face in her hands, she looked straight into my eyes and said, "Be kind, and be happy." Ever since, as much as I can, I try to embody this in my own life. Over time, I have come to realize that this is the deal with compassion: It's not that we somehow have to make ourselves be kind and make ourselves be happy because we know it's how we "should" be. It's that being kind, to ourselves and to others, makes us happy. I went to Katmandu out of a sense of duty to my family and because my teacher told me to. I hardly recognized it as an act of kindness for myself. But when I met my grandmother, I saw things differently. In a way, compassion cultivation training is my attempt to codify and "translate" for the rest of us what came so naturally to my grandmother.

It comes back to connection

No doubt there are individual differences in how naturally self-compassion comes to each of us, based on the kind of parenting we received and other factors, possibly including our genetic predisposition. The two keys going forward, however—the things we can change—are how we define ourselves as individuals and the sense of connection we feel with others. Of course, the stronger our sense of separateness, the weaker our feeling of connection with others. And the less we feel connected with others, paradoxically, the less we feel connected with ourselves. We can end up disconnected from our own feelings, needs, and joys.

I remember reading about a study after the economic crisis of 2008 that showed that people who identified too strongly or exclusively with their jobs were less resilient when they lost their jobs than people who put their sense of identity and worth in more than one basket, such as fatherhood (the study participants were men), marriage, friendship, community, and so on. (When we put it this way, it doesn't sound so paradoxical.) When the men who felt more connected to others took a blow in one area of their identity, even though it was an important one, they had enough other scaffolding to hold up their overall sense of worth, and so they functioned better. This, of course, gave them the added advantage of a more optimistic frame of mind and constructive attitude, which helped them respond more effectively when new opportunities came their way. In contrast, those who had isolated their identity in their work experienced more feelings of inadequacy, bitterness, and diminished self-worth. And though they may have felt alone, they didn't suffer alone; their spouses, children, and others who cared for them suffered by seeing their loved one undergo such psychological and emotional pain.

Cultural psychologists tell us how our cultures shape our

sense of who we are—our sense of self—and how our selves define our interaction with the world around us.[9] Though each one of us has multiple dimensions of self, they fall into two basic styles: independent and interdependent selves. Some experts assert that our optimal well-being can be found in a healthy combination of the two. Other studies suggest that having a sense of self that is more interdependent than independent, more complex than simple, and more fluid than fixed leads to greater psychological health, including greater resilience and happiness. Either way, the connection that we as individuals feel with others is essential. It's no wonder that psychologists rank social connection—a person's subjective sense of affectionate and loving connection with others—as a primary need once basic physiological and safety requirements are met.

In one sense, the challenge of self-compassion is straightforward. It asks us to bring a genuine sense of caring to our experience and respond to it with understanding, acceptance, and kindness. This is what we do when we respond compassionately to the needs and suffering of a loved one—nothing more, nothing mysterious. If it happens more naturally for others, then our compassion training can start there. In Part II of the book, I offer specific practices that we use in our Stanford program, aimed at training the heart and mind to be more predisposed toward greater self-compassion.

3

From Fear to Courage

Breaking Through Our Resistance

*Dwelling on the past brings remorseful thoughts and clinging
to future so let go of it.
Clinging to future increases our hopes and fears so let go of it.*

—Yangönpa (1213–58)

*I learned that courage was not the absence of fear, but the tri-
umph over it.*

—Nelson Mandela (1918–2013)

We need other people's kindness most when we are feeling vulnerable. But for many of us, this is also the time when we are
not very good at seeking help and benefiting from it. At these
crucial moments we are often overcome by fear, defensiveness,
and pride. When this happens, we not only prevent ourselves
from benefiting from others' help and kindness; we also block
expressions of that gentler, wiser, and kinder part of ourselves.

The courage of compassion

I was thirty-six when I made the choice to leave the monastic life. By then, I had become a source of pride for the Tibetan monastic establishment, and for the members of my own Ganden Shartse monastery in particular. I was the Dalai Lama's English translator, a scholar of Buddhist thought with many students at the monastery, and someone who seemed to stand as a "proof" that the ancient monastic life and modern knowledge can coexist without conflict. I had been a monk for more than two decades, since the age of eleven; the monastery was my home and fellow monks were my family, my friends, and my community. It was my anchor and my world. To leave it was to leave behind everything that had given me strength, joy, and meaning. It was the scariest thing I have done in my life.

What was I so afraid of and why? There was, of course, the fear of leaving the familiar and venturing into the unknown. This fear was, I noticed, tinged with curiosity, as I wondered what the world might hold. Would it reveal aspects of my personality that had been hidden in a monastic life? There was also the fear of how others might judge me, especially my monastic colleagues and the Tibetan community as a whole. Would they see this as a betrayal? Would they be disappointed in me? How would my father take the news? How would this affect my relationship with His Holiness the Dalai Lama? Such were the thoughts that occupied my mind.

Inevitably, when we are part of a close-knit community, be it a monastery of four hundred or a household of two, others will be affected by any major change we make. It's natural for family members to invest their feelings and identities in each other's achievements and failures, and I cannot blame people for doing the same with me. I recognized that my decision would affect my life and that I alone was responsible for my actions. Still, there was the moral question of my responsibility to my community. Would it be selfish to leave? What about the pain I would cause the many individuals I respected and cared about deeply (and, to this day, still do)?

The first step, I realized, was to be absolutely sure about my choice. The reason I needed to leave was the yearning I felt for a family of my own. This may have had something to do with being separated from my family so early in life and losing my mother when I was a child. Whatever was behind it, the feeling had been there for some time, and never really went away. If anything, it grew as the years went by. And no matter how hard I tried, I could not visualize myself as a white-haired, elderly monk in maroon robes. So, through some deep reflection, it became clear that it was no longer a question of *if*, but of *when* and *how*. I also realized that the sooner I left, the less damage I would likely do. Though I was a senior monastic member, I had not yet held any important office, such as the abbotship. If I was going to leave, I needed to do it soon.

Then I realized that fearing how others might judge me was the wrong thing to worry about. In any case, there wasn't much I could do about this. Instead I could be thinking about how to minimize the damage my leaving might cause. I wanted people to understand that my decision had nothing to do with disillusionment with the tradition; it concerned only my private life. I profoundly admire the ideal behind the

monastic life—to dedicate one's life to the pursuit of meditative training, knowledge, and the service of others is truly
noble. Somehow I needed to communicate this to my fellow
monastics. So I went back to Cambridge, this time to pursue a
PhD in religious studies. I wanted to give myself and the community time and space, to make the break easier for both sides.
(A second reason was to make myself more employable, since
I would now need to make a living like everybody else.)

Once my monastic colleagues came to know my reason for
leaving, they were very understanding. I was also most fortunate to meet my future wife, Sophie, soon after I decided to
leave. So things fell into place, making the transition reasonably smooth. My kind colleagues and friends at the monastery
were relieved to know that the break had not been too trau-
matic for me. The painful part came when I visited as a
layperson for the first time, dressed in ordinary clothes. When
my former students came to see me, many of them cried. This
was really hard. I assured them my dedication to serve Tibet's
classical culture remained as strong as ever.

My father took the news remarkably well. I was surprised,
since he was normally so worried about what other people
might think. My two siblings' reactions could not have been
more different. When I called them to share the news, one
said, "This is so embarrassing! How am I going to show my face
to others?" The other said, "Why did you wait so long? If you
had left earlier it would have been easier to adapt to the new
life." I knew their reactions had more to do with them than
with me.

The Dalai Lama's response was another story. A few months
after I had made the announcement, his office called me to say

that my presence was needed during a visit to Switzerland. I told the secretary that since I was no longer a monk we could not assume that things would continue as before. He assured me that the suggestion came from the Dalai Lama himself.

I must admit that I was nervous about appearing to His Holiness in lay clothes, with my "long" (unshaved) hair. Up until then, I had always met with the Dalai Lama as a fellow monastic, dressed similarly in the maroon robes typical of Tibetan monks. The Dalai Lama was staying at a Tibetan monastery not far from Zurich. As I walked into his room, His Holiness laughed and joked about how I looked quite smart in trousers. That broke the ice. He also told me, "You always had a slightly large head. Now with hair, your head looks even more impressive." Feeling somewhat more relaxed, I apologized for not being able to continue to serve him and the world as a monk. The Dalai Lama replied, "I would be lying if I said that, as a monastic, I am not saddened to lose a fellow monk. However, I know you well. I know you have not made this decision lightly and I trust your judgment."

His Holiness went on to give me some personal advice. He said that although he is no expert, he has seen far too many people get entangled in complicated relationships. Not only does this then become a source of pain and acrimony; it leaves little emotional and attentional space to do much good for themselves and others. Most importantly, he advised, I should not have children before I was sure that I had met the right partner. Separation and divorce causes so much pain and confusion to innocent children, he said. I was touched to hear this advice on family life coming from a monk, and even more so from the Dalai Lama himself. We both knew that neither of us had any experience with courting or marriage or parenthood, but he had gone out of his way to offer me these heartfelt observations from his experience with so many people over the years.

All of this reinforced for me some of the important insights of the Buddhist teachings on compassion. First, when we face a challenge, if we remain caught within the narrow confines of self-preoccupation then fear becomes the dominant emotion. Fear of being judged, fear of being disliked, fear of being seen as a disappointment, fear of being rejected—these will take over our thoughts and feelings. Although it's human to react in such terms, fear usually only complicates matters when it becomes our primary motive. Fear disconnects us from our natural capacity to empathize and we become unavailable for others. As for how others might judge us, what can we do about it, anyway? Generally, it's good to care about what others think. It's part of what makes us moral creatures. However, worrying too much is counterproductive. If we let fear rule our lives we become paralyzed. In the end, it's a question of balance: self-compassion to take care of our needs, and compassion for others to avoid stepping on theirs.

When we focus on our concern for others' well-being, our attitude shifts to "How might this action of mine affect those who care about me?" "How can I minimize the feeling of hurt it might engender?" "Is there something I can do to reassure my loved ones?" Not only will there be fewer negative feelings; there will also be less stress and heaviness because of the absence of self-agenda. This lets us be more proactive, redirecting our energy to communicating to our loved ones in a way that will reassure them. In the end, when people understand the reasons why we chose to do something, and when they get the basic message that we don't want to hurt them, they tend to be more accepting of our decisions and compassionate toward us. This is human nature.

The Dalai Lama's response to my change in life also reminded me to be sensitive to the specific needs of a given situation. Especially in intimate relationships, there will be times when one side feels more vulnerable than the other. It helps if the one who is less vulnerable offers kindness and understanding rather than judgment and recrimination. When someone is already feeling uncertain and scared, "What were you thinking? I told you so," is the least helpful thing to say. Even if we might be right, sometimes it's not the right time to be right. There is a saying in Tibetan, just as in English, that we should not kick someone who is already down, nor penalize someone who has already been punished.

Compassion—for ourselves and for others—takes courage. It takes courage to take care of ourselves, to make decisions in our best interest and not let our fear of what other people think throw us off course. It also takes courage to care what people think, to have compassion for the effects of our actions on others. Compassion requires us to pay attention and engage with people's troubles and suffering when it might be easier to ignore them or to otherwise make do with the status quo. It takes courage to trust enough to open ourselves up to others, whether in asking for or offering help. People who are suffering are not always on their best behavior! It takes courage to lower our defenses and reach out to people where they are, to have compassion anyway.

However, compassion also *makes* courage. Acting out of

compassion for ourselves, we can be more confident that we are doing the right thing. At the same time, having compassion for others frees us from fearing for ourselves. It turns our attention outward, expanding our perspective, making our own problems seem smaller in the scheme of things, or not like "our own" problems at all, but part of something bigger than us that we are all in together. We feel stronger when we realize the "others" we have been fearing are really on the same team; compassion hinges on this realization. It takes courage to open our hearts to others and expose our vulnerability, but as the Dalai Lama often points out, when we do we feel transparent and free. We can stop hiding, stop fearing someone will see who we really are, because we are choosing to be seen.

Fear of compassion

Compassion sounds like such a nice thing, so what are we afraid of? Our fear—or fears, rather, since it comes in different kinds—is among the intriguing findings that have emerged from the new science of compassion.[1] Paul Gilbert, a British psychiatrist and pioneer in compassion-based therapy, first schematized fear of compassion in the clinical setting. He found that many of his patients who suffer from high shame and pathological self-criticism possess a gut-level resistance to compassion.[2] Unless this fear is first addressed, Gilbert discovered, direct exposure to therapies that explicitly induce compassion might not be helpful. He identified three kinds of fear of compassion: fear of compassion *for others*, *from others*, and *for oneself*. He helped to develop self-report measures for each of these three kinds of fear. For example, with relation to compassion for others, how strongly do we identify with the following statements?

- People will take advantage of me if I am too compassionate and forgiving.

- If I am too compassionate others will become dependent on me.

- I can't tolerate others' distress.

- People should help themselves rather than waiting for others to help them.

- There are some people in life who don't deserve compassion.

With relation to fear of compassion from others:

- I am afraid that if I need other people to be kind they will not be so.

- I worry that people are only kind and compassionate when they want something from me.

- If I think someone is being kind and caring toward me, I put up a barrier.

And with relation to fear of compassion for oneself:

- I fear that if I develop compassion for myself, I will become someone I don't want to be.

- I fear that if I am more self-compassionate I will become weak.

- I fear that if I start to feel compassion for myself, I will be overcome with sadness and grief.[3]

Each of us can recognize ourselves in some or all of these fears. This suggests that some degree of resistance toward compassion is as natural as the arising of compassion itself.

To a large extent, these fears stem from confusing compassion with submissiveness, weakness, or sentimentality. But they are unfounded. Compassion does not preclude standing up for ourselves when we are being treated unfairly. If a colleague at work attempts to discredit us so that he might get the promotion instead, we could retaliate—spread nasty rumors about him, yell at him, and so forth. Alternatively, we could recognize where his behavior is coming from. Often, unskillful, unkind behavior comes from insecurity rooted in jealousy. Clearly, in this case, there is misguided self-interest and shortsightedness at work too. We can remember, when we have the urge to make this person suffer, that he is already suffering. The moment you can empathize with your colleague, you'll be in a better position to maintain composure and respond to the situation with calm and clarity. You might approach him and try to talk to him, tell him you think you understand. You might say that you think he, for his part, will understand why you are asking him to stop. He might surprise you by understanding.

Having compassion for others doesn't mean people aren't accountable for their actions. We might think that some people simply don't deserve our compassion. The larger question of how compassion relates to justice is beyond the scope of this book. That said, much of the tension we perceive stems from misunderstanding compassion and forgiveness. Having compassion for perpetrators of injustice doesn't mean that we condone their actions, and it doesn't prevent us from confronting them. If anything, it lets us deal with the situation more efficiently, without the costs of anger and enmity. It means we never lose sight of the fact that these individuals are human beings too, and, just like us, they are trying to avoid suffering and find happiness. Even as we hold people accountable and do what we can to stop injustice, we can remember their humanity, and not lose sight of their perspective and needs. As the Dalai Lama often reminds us, forgiving someone does not mean forgetting what he or she has done.[4] If we have forgotten, there is nothing to forgive. Forgiveness is for the person, not for his or her deeds. This simple idea is powerfully captured in the Christian injunction that we should love the sinner but hate the sin.

Another common fear is that someone might become too dependent on us. Behind that fear, we can usually find a false belief that compassion means doing everything for that person. In fact, the most compassionate thing we can do is to help empower others to draw from their own inner resources— teach a person to fish instead of giving him a fish, as the saying goes. Helping others help themselves is one of the highest forms of compassion.

We might also resist compassion out of fear that we won't be able to cope with another person's distress, since compassion involves opening ourselves to others' suffering (and don't we feel stressed enough already?). This fear may come from not knowing what to do when we're confronted with a problem that cannot be fixed. Many of us, especially men, are uncomfortable with problems that have no clear solution. Compassion acknowledges the fundamental truth of our human condition that not all pain can be fixed, and that there is a limit to what each of us can do in the face of suffering. It calls for an attitude of humility. In many situations, it's not fixing that is needed; rather, it's our empathic response, our acceptance, understanding, and solidarity. Sometimes, someone just needs a "yeah, that sucks," or a hug. In any case, it's always helpful to remember that some pain and sorrow are unavoidable, part of what it means to be human. It's not up to us to say *whether*, but we can choose how we respond. Do we resist the reality of suffering with anger, denial, or detachment? Are we gripped with thoughts like "Why me?" or "It's not fair!" or "I can't deal with this," which only add suffering on top of suffering? Or can we respond with understanding, compassion, and courage? This is our choice.

A sixty-seven-year-old man in our compassion cultivation training told us the following story about the courage he found in compassion:

"I often go to a sandwich shop for lunch. I always avoided a disheveled young man at the door asking for money. Ignoring these people on street corners and outside of markets seemed to be the best way of dealing with the begging. In about the fourth week of CCT, to my surprise, I found myself looking directly at him: "I don't give out money but I will be glad to buy you a sandwich." We waited in line; he got his sandwich and thanked me as he left. The next time I saw him there I offered to buy him a sandwich and join me

for lunch if he wanted. 'Sure, dude.' I got to know this homeless nineteen-year-old's story, his courage in being on the
streets, his gratitude for a moment of kindness. I still feel like
he gave me a gift. Something has happened as I have practiced compassion training. My heart is gradually opening
and my courage growing. People everywhere, once strangers,
have become real to me. I am working to understand better
what the Dalai Lama means when he says, 'I have never met
anyone who is a stranger.'"[5]

Pride: the false guard

Pride is another common inhibitor of compassion. It mas-
querades as strength, but it is really another kind of fear. As we
saw in the previous chapter, many of us invest our identities
heavily in performance and success. We live under great pressure to prove ourselves. So when things don't go the way we
planned or expected, we are reluctant to reach out for help,
especially from the people whose opinions matter the most to
us. Pride gets in the way, followed by feelings such as shame,
guilt, and bitterness. Rather than admit our need and seek
help, we put up a facade, tough it out, and suffer alone.

Pride can be particularly harmful when it becomes a barrier
in the aftermath of a conflict in close relations—between cou-
ples, between a parent and child, between friends. Blocking the
way to compassion and reconciliation, pride allows the negative experience of conflict to fester. It creates a vicious cycle,
while each side waits defensively for the other to make the first
move. In this dynamic, statements such as "I'm sorry" and "I

love you" that express our deeper feelings don't come easily, but they are just the words we need. Here we can learn something from how children make up after a fight. Small children don't dwell on the conflict; they move on. They don't suffer from the pain of injured pride like we adults do. Pride turns small bruises into deep, self-inflicted wounds. In this way, it is a false guard.

In pride, we confuse haughtiness with standing firm on principle. We confuse taking the initiative to reconcile with meekness and giving in. In reality, it is always more helpful to reach out to the other person, even when we might be in the right. My wife and I agreed at the beginning of our relationship that we would never go to bed angry. This way, no matter how harsh an argument may have been, it can never be older than a day. This practice has proved to be a powerful antidote against pride, preventing it from becoming a barrier in our relationship.

A culture of kindness

Contemporary culture resists compassion in some ways too. Individual autonomy is so prized that we may experience concern and need for others as signs of weakness. To protect ourselves, we internalize a tough self-image with harsh statements like "Dependence is weakness," "I don't need others," and "I don't let others in so I won't get hurt." There is nothing wrong with feeling independent per se. Problems arise when we take it to the extreme and end up alienated from our basic nature as social, interconnected beings with needs that are universal to our condition.

In traditional Tibetan culture, kindness is highly valued, and Tibetans learn from an early age to give and receive it more easily. People appreciate kindness from others instead of fearing it, with the assumption that interdependence is natural for humans. Visitors to Tibet often remark on the generous hospitality—how Tibetans openly invite strangers into their homes and serve them tea and food. Perhaps this has something to do with the reality of life on the Tibetan Plateau, where people have lived for many centuries in small numbers spread across a vast, geographically challenging land. So, when I first noticed that in the West people sometimes have a gut reluctance—or even aversion—to receiving kindness, it came as a bit of a shock. I have seen people react to kindness as if it were an insult. I remember in my first year as a student in Cambridge, I offered my help to an elderly gentleman with a walking stick who was crossing a street. He looked back at me with annoyance, as if he was offended. Perhaps my intrusion reminded him of his old age, which he did not like to think about. Later I observed that some people don't want to feel indebted to another person.

Letting go of our resistance

One way or another, the inhibitors of compassion are forms of resistance we bring to our everyday experience, especially as we encounter difficulty, pain, and sorrow. We use fear, defensiveness, pride, or, when we turn our gaze away, simple suppression to protect ourselves from hurting. Resistance may serve well to protect us when the challenges are physical. Faced with a mugger or a saber-toothed tiger, we either fight back in self-defense or flee. But the fight-or-flight reaction doesn't help when it comes to mental and emotional challenges. In fact, our resistance opens the door to further suffering. This ancient Buddhist understanding—that our resistance makes things worse—represents a powerful insight into the nature of human suffering.

I found a Western analogy for this when, as an adult, I learned to downhill ski. At first, my body was stiff with fear. (A local journalist discovered that falling on ice is new immigrants' greatest fear when they first come to live in Montreal, my own home as well since 1999.) It was only when I let go of the stiffness and relaxed that I began to get good at it. I also learned that when you fall, letting your body relax and go with the fall minimizes injury. This seemed paradoxical at first.

The instinct to resist (falling or suffering) comes from fundamental human drives. We all have a basic urge for security—something solid to hold on to, stable ground that we can trustfully stand on. We instinctively seek control, predictability, and resolution, and we are uncomfortable with uncertainty and change. But no matter how hard we try, we can never eliminate uncertainty and change in our lives.

Plus, our natural dislike of change is aggravated by the radical uncertainties that characterize contemporary life. Even before the digital age, the poet W. H. Auden described the post-industrial period as the "age of anxiety." Many of the institutions that provided constancy and anchored traditional societies—church, monarchy, and strong community—no longer play crucial roles for people in the modern world. In our digital age almost everything seems to be up for grabs. There is little attachment to "home" in the physical sense; fewer people have an emotional connection to where they come from. People experience security and stability less and less in their jobs, and corporate culture is defined by shareholder returns within the shortest time cycle.

One of the first spiritual insights the Buddha shared with his disciples was the truth of impermanence. The pain of losing what we have, not finding what we desire, getting what we do not want, these are part and parcel of what it means to live, the Buddha reminds us. They are essential aspects of our common human experience; they do not come about because somehow we have failed to get things right. And our happiness lies not in avoiding pain and sorrow, but in not letting them disturb our basic equilibrium—the calm of allowing, at least for the moment, the way things are. The sooner we make friends with them, the sooner we can stop reacting and start living with compassion for ourselves and for others. I must admit that this is a difficult truth to accept, no matter how true it might be. Hopefully, when we see how much harder it is to fight it we can agree that acceptance, understanding, patience, and kindness—compassion—is worth the effort to try. Compassion cultivation training, in Part II of this book, is designed to help.

We could try to protect ourselves against uncertainty and change by controlling our environment, the behavior of other people, and the whole world. This is not, however, a realistic strategy. Alternatively, we could change ourselves and adapt to the reality we find ourselves in. Shantideva, the eighth-century Indian Buddhist author whose seminal text I memorized as a young monk, offers another analogy: If we were to try to cover the entire face of the earth with leather to protect our feet, where could we find enough leather? Instead, by covering the soles of our feet with leather shoes we can achieve the same purpose as covering the entire earth.[6] The best solution to a problem is the one that you yourself can bring about.

Building our compassion muscle: compassion cultivation at Stanford University

The vision behind our Stanford compassion training is an ambitious one. We aim not merely to bring attention to compassion as a central human value or make ourselves more empathetic toward others. Rather, the aim is to offer a systematic practice to make compassion the fundamental principle governing all aspects of our lives, from how we see ourselves and interact with others, to bringing up our children, to engaging with the world around us. When left untrained, our experience of compassion tends to be reactive: Compassion arises in response to the suffering or need of someone we love. In the case of a stranger or an animal suffering, it takes that much more to provoke our compassion. Through training, however, we can make compassion our basic stance, the very outlook with which we perceive ourselves and the world around us, so that we engage with the world from that place.

There is an intimate and dynamic link between how we *perceive* ourselves, others, and the world around us on the one hand and how we *experience* them on the other. This, in turn, influences how we *act*. In other words, our emotions define our behavior; and our thoughts and perceptions—our attitudes, outlook, and attendant values—determine how we experience our world. For instance, if we see the world as a dangerous place and others as uncaring and self-serving, we relate to them primarily out of fear, suspicion, rivalry, and antagonism. In contrast, if we see the world as generally a joyful place and others as basically caring people, we then experience the world around us with a sense of trust, belonging, and security. How diametrically different the lived world can be for two individuals in exactly the same neighborhood and with the same socioeconomic status, simply because of their opposing perspectives! By changing the way we perceive ourselves and the world we live in, we can transform the way we experience ourselves and the world. This is what the Buddha meant when he stated, "With our thoughts we make the world."[7] And this is the theory of transformation behind compassion cultivation training developed at Stanford.

In CCT, we target four areas for change: outlook, awareness, capacity for empathy, and behavior. We change our outlook primarily by working with our conscious intentions and the attitudes we bring to our everyday experience of the world. We enhance our awareness by working at our attentional capacity and learning simply to be with our own experiences as they unfold. We cultivate our empathic capacity by warming our hearts through consciously wishing others well, especially our loved ones, and taking joy in their happiness. We learn to expand the scope of our empathy by recognizing similarities that we share with others, especially our common humanity. Through changing our outlook, awareness, and capacity for empathy, and by consciously living out our compassion in action, we transform our behavior. Through changing our behavior, we change the world.

You can guess from Chapter 2 that a critical target of transformation in our training is what we might call our self-to-self relationship. A healthy and compassionate relationship with ourselves, in which we relate to our own situation with kindness, understanding, and genuine acceptance, is the seafloor to anchor our relationship with others and with the world around us. So cultivating self-compassion is an important focus, both at Stanford and in the next part of this book.

In the next five chapters of the book, I present the key elements of our Stanford compassion training, including the specific meditation practices associated with each step. Beginning with setting conscious intentions, we learn to focus our attention and bring greater awareness to our own experiences. We then practice warming our hearts so that we more easily connect with others, especially our loved ones. Once we have laid the groundwork through cultivating our intention, attention, and empathy, we turn to the challenge of cultivating self-compassion. Finally, with self-compassion and self-kindness firmly anchored, we work on expanding our circle of concern so that, at least in aspiration, it embraces all humanity. As an important step to enlarging this circle, we cultivate genuine feelings of connection with others, through embracing a gut-level recognition of our shared aspiration for happiness.

We must address our fears if we are to overcome resistance to compassion. The next part of this book will help you explore the personal beliefs underpinning yours. You will see how resistance to compassion, including self-compassion, manifests in your thoughts, attitudes, and emotional reactions, and you will learn how to deal with these through awareness and understanding. Through practice we can learn to be with our uncertainty and respond flexibly to our experiences of pain, sorrow, and fear—not fighting them and resisting them; rather, observing them, being with them, and responding with gentle understanding. This is a radically different approach to life. It asks us to change our habitual self-protective patterns. It calls for a fearless heart. It asks us to be comfortable in the midst of uncertainty, to feel secure even when the ground beneath us is shifting all the time. This is, however, a response we have to learn. It requires a new outlook on our part. It calls for a different set of attitudes with respect to our experience. And it demands a different way of relating to ourselves and to the world around us. This is what transformational practices like mindfulness and compassion training can teach us.

As we saw in Chapter 1, your capacity—and courage—for compassion is already in you. It's a matter of clearing the way.

Part II

Training Our Mind and Heart

4

From Compassion to Action
Turning Intention into Motivation

Good and bad karma are functions of the mind ...
all our actions are defined by our intention.

—Tsongkhapa (1357–1419)

Anyone can see that intending and not acting when we can is
not really intending, and loving and not doing good when we
can is not really loving.

—Emanuel Swedenborg (1688–1772), *Heaven and Hell*

May all beings attain happiness and its causes.
May all beings be free from suffering and its causes.
May all beings never be separated from joy that is free of
*   misery.*
May all beings abide in equanimity, free from bias of
*   attachment and aversion.*

I fondly remember waking up as a child in smoky tents in a remote part of northern India, near Shimla, to the undulating sound of my mother chanting these lines, among other prayers, as she churned Tibetan butter tea for breakfast. The churning of butter tea inside a *dongmo*, a vertical wooden tube held together by copper bands, with the up-and-down motion of a long stick attached to a wooden disk, makes a soothing, repetitive, gushing noise. The tent camps where my parents lived as road workers would move sites, but the children's village where I was boarding would arrange for us to visit our parents a week or two at a time. Later, growing up, I came to treasure these memories of my mother, and her chanting of the Four Immeasurables prayer made those memories all the more meaningful.

The four immeasurables

Compassion is one of the "four immeasurables," as reflected by the second line of this prayer: *May all beings be free from suffering and its causes*. The other three are loving-kindness, sympathetic joy, and equanimity. Informally speaking, these are the qualities that, according to Buddhist psychology, you can never have too much of. As with compassion, we all have these qualities; they're part of—the best parts of—being human. So, while you may not be familiar with all the terms, you know what they are: Loving-kindness is love with no strings attached, just the pure wish for someone to be happy (not least, ourselves)—*May all beings attain happiness and its causes*. Sympathetic joy is experiencing happiness at someone else's happiness or good fortune—*May all beings never be separated from joy that is free of misery.* Equanimity is staying calm no matter what life throws at us—pleasure and pain, likes and dislikes, success and failure, praise and blame, fame and disrepute—and it lets us relate to everyone as human beings, beyond the categories of friend, foe, or stranger. The Buddha made a telling *mudra*, or gesture, as he sat under a tree becoming enlightened, in which he touched one hand to the ground to signal that whatever storm of troubles raged around him, whatever provocations came at him, he would hold his spot. This is the picture of equanimity. *May all beings abide in equanimity, free from bias of attachment and aversion.*

Each of these qualities, also known as the "sublime abidings," has an opposite, or "far enemy," that is obvious enough. For compassion, it's cruelty; for loving-kindness, ill will or harmful intent; for sympathetic joy, envy or jealousy. (Worse still, envy or jealousy may lead us to take joy in the misfortune of someone we do not like. I remember how conflicted I felt when, in 1976, the Tibetan refugee communities in India erupted in celebration at the news of Chairman Mao's death. If there is one person who was most responsible for the suffering of the Tibetan people—the annexation of Tibet, the suppression of its people, the destruction of its culture and ecology—and whose tragic legacies remain still unresolved, it's the great helmsman of Communist China. As a restless teenager, I might have liked to join in the celebrations, but my monastic training made me think better of it. I did, however, enjoy the holiday we had from our routine of study and fieldwork at the monastery.) Equanimity has a few opposites: greed, aversion, and prejudice, which together cause so much agitation in our mind and undermine its equilibrium.

Less obvious are the "near enemies," or mental states similar enough to the immeasurables that they can easily be confused, but they are equal causes of needless suffering. As we cultivate the good qualities, we must be on the lookout for these impostors. Loving-kindness's near enemy is selfish affection or attachment, as when we love someone for what we think they can give us. Sympathetic joy's near enemy is frivolous joy, which grasps at pleasant but meaningless experiences. Equanimity's near enemy is indifference or apathy, the critical difference is that equanimity is engaged— we don't stop caring, but we do stay calm. With equanimity, we are free from the habitual forces of expectation and apprehension that make us so vulnerable to over-excitation and disappointment.

Compassion's near enemy is pity. Unlike genuine compassion, pity implies a sense of superiority. So, unlike compassion, which connects us with the object of our concern because we identify, pity distances us from the other person. Compassion includes respect: We honor the other person's dignity as a fellow human being. Our concern, if it comes from genuine compassion, is based on the recognition that, *just like I do*, this person wishes to be free from suffering.

In traditional Buddhist meditations on loving-kindness and compassion, we typically begin by connecting compassionately with our own experience, especially the experience of suffering, and with our natural aspirations for happiness. Then, focusing on a loved one, we consciously wish him or her joy, happiness, and peace, by silently offering phrases such as "May you be happy; may you find peace and joy." From there, in an ever-expanding circle, we wish joy, happiness, and peace for a neutral person, then for a difficult person, and finally moving toward the largest circle, wishing joy, happiness, and peace for all beings. In meditation on loving-kindness we wish others happiness; in meditation on compassion we wish others to be free of suffering. Then, to counter our tendencies toward envy or discomfort at other people's good fortune, we cultivate sympathetic joy. Finally, to rise above our biases rooted in discriminating emotions of attachment and hostility ("I like this ... I don't like that ... I like her ... I don't like *her* ..."), we cultivate equanimity.

In the Tibetan tradition, we recognize compassion as both the highest spiritual ideal and the highest expression of our humanity. Even the Tibetan word for compassion, *nyingjé*, which literally means the "king of heart," captures the priority we accord compassion. It's this Tibetan compassion meditation tradition that I have used as the primary resource in developing both the basic framework and the specific guided meditations for the Stanford compassion training.

Setting conscious intention

In our compassion training, we begin every session with a practice called *setting your intention*. This is a contemplative exercise adapted from traditional Tibetan meditation, a kind of checking-in, in which we connect with our deeper aspirations so that they may inform our intentions and motivations. Thus connected, we compose a set of thoughts to form the background from which our subsequent thoughts and emotions may emerge.

In everyday English, we often use the two words, *intention* and *motivation*, interchangeably as if they mean the same thing, but there's an important difference: deliberateness. Our motivation to do something is the reason or reasons behind that behavior, the source of our desire, and the drive to do it. We may be more or less aware of our motivation. Psychologists define motivation as the process that "arouses, sustains, and regulates human and animal behavior." Simply put, motivation is what turns us on. For some it might be fame; for others it might be money; excitement or thrill; sex; recognition; loyalty; service; a sense of belonging, safety, justice; and so on. The force of motivation develops through a mutually reinforcing cycle of desire and reward—when something we do is rewarding, we want to do it again; if we do it again, we are rewarded again, and want to do it more . . .

Intention, on the other hand, is always deliberate, an articulation of a conscious goal. Intention is necessarily conscious; motivation, as Freud pointed out, need not be conscious even to the person herself. We need intentions for the long view. We set and reaffirm our best intentions to keep us inclining in the direction we truly mean to go. But we need motivation to keep us going over the long haul. If our intention is to run a marathon, there will be times, when the alarm clock goes off for a ten-mile run before work, or in the middle of running, when we'll ask ourselves, quite reasonably, "*Why* am I doing this?" We need good, inspired answers to get us over such humps. Conscious or unconscious, motivation is the why, and the spark, behind intention.

You could do this intention-setting exercise at home, first thing in the morning if that is convenient. You could also do it on a bus or train during your commute. If you work in an office, you could do it sitting at your desk before you get into the day. You only need two to five uninterrupted minutes. The Tibetan tradition recommends setting our intention and checking with our motivations in this manner at the beginning of the day, at the start of a meditation sitting, and before any important activity. Our intention sets the tone for whatever we are about to do. Like music, intention can influence our mood, thoughts, and feelings—setting an intention in the morning, we set the tone for the day.

EXERCISE: Setting an Intention

First, find a comfortable sitting posture. If you can, sit on a cushion on the floor or on a chair with the soles of your feet touching the ground, which gives you a feeling of being grounded. If you prefer, you could also lie down on your back, ideally on a surface that is not too soft. Once you have found your posture, relax your body as much as you can, if necessary with some stretches, especially your shoulders and your back.

Then, with your eyes closed if it helps you to focus, take three to five deep, diaphragmatic or abdominal breaths, each time drawing the inhalation down into the belly and filling up the torso with the in-breath from the bottom to the top, like filling a jar with water. Then with a long, slow exhalation, expel all the air from the torso. If it helps, you can exhale from your mouth. Inhale ... and exhale ...

Once you feel settled, contemplate the following questions: "What is it that I value deeply? What, in the depth of my heart, do I wish for myself, for my loved ones, and for the world?"

Stay on these questions a little and see if any answers come up. If no specific answers surface, don't worry; simply stay with the open questions. This may take some getting used to, since in the West, when we are asked questions we usually expect to answer them. Trust that the questions themselves are working, even—or especially—when we don't have ready answers. If and when answers do come up, acknowledge them as they arise, and stay with whatever thoughts and feelings they may bring.

Finally, develop a specific set of thoughts as your conscious intention—for this day, for instance. You could think, "Today, may I be more mindful of my body, mind, and speech in my interaction with others. May I, as far as I can, avoid deliberately hurting others. May I relate to myself, to others, and to the events around me with kindness, understanding, and less judgment. May I use my day in a way that is in tune with my deeper values."

In this way, set the tone for the day.

* * *

Once we become more familiar with intention setting, we can do this practice in a minute or less. That means we can find opportunities during the day to check in with our intentions. Doctors who have taken compassion training, for example, have used the time it takes to wash their hands between patients to return to their intentions,[1] and report how this makes them feel more centered and present for the next patient. We can even skip the three-phase formal practice and do a quick reset by reading or chanting a few meaningful lines. You could use the Four Immeasurables prayer:

May all beings attain happiness and its causes.
May all beings be free from suffering and its causes.
May all beings never be separated from joy that is free of
    misery.
May all beings abide in equanimity, free from bias of
    attachment and aversion.

Dedicating our experience

The intention-setting practice is paired, in Tibetan tradition, with another contemplative exercise called *dedication*. The role of this exercise is to complete the circle, as it were. At the end of a day, or a meditation, or any other effort we have made, we reconnect with the intentions we set at the beginning, reflecting on our experience in light of our intentions and rejoicing in what we have achieved. This is like taking stock at the end of the day. It gives us another opportunity to connect with our deeper aspirations.

EXERCISE: Making a Dedication

At the end of day—for instance, before you go to bed or as you lie in bed before sleeping—reflect on your day.

Briefly review the events of the day (including significant conversations, moods, and other mental activity) and touch back on the spirit of the morning intention-setting exercise. See how much alignment there is between the two. It's important not to get caught up in the details of what you did and did not do. The idea is not to keep exhaustive scores, but to broadly survey to see the synergy between your intentions and your life that day.

Whatever thoughts and feelings this reviewing might bring, just stay with them. There's no need to push them away if they have a negative quality, or grasp at them if they seem positive. Simply stay with it for a while in silence.

Finally, think of something from the day that you feel good about—a helping hand you gave your neighbor, an empathetic ear you lent a colleague in distress, not losing your cool in the pharmacy when someone barged in front of you. Then take joy in the thought of this deed. If nothing else, take joy in the fact that you began your day by setting a conscious intention.

* * *

Keep this exercise short; three to five minutes is a good length. If you normally do some reading before bed, you could set aside three to five minutes at the end for dedication time. If your habit is to watch TV, could you watch three to five minutes less? Or go somewhere quiet during commercials? Taking joy in the day, at the end of the day, even in the simple fact of the effort we have made, is important. It gives us something positive to carry into the next day, and helps us harness motivation in the service of our intentions. As we shall see later in the chapter, joy plays a crucial role in our motivation, especially in sustaining motivation over a prolonged period of time.

Sometimes, however, it's helpful to do a more focused review. This is especially true if we are struggling with a particular issue or are engaged in some endeavor, such as an eight-week compassion training course! Each week in CCT we work on certain qualities and attitudes we seek to foster. Say, for example, one week it's self-compassion. During this period, we set intentions around being kinder to ourselves. In turn, at the end of a day, our dedication might pay special attention to kindnesses we may have shown ourselves that day.

Now, when we undertake such a targeted assessment, most of us will find that we fall short. We will see the gaps between our intentions and our behavior, between our aspirations and our actual life. When this happens, it's important not to beat ourselves with negative judgment and self-criticism. We simply acknowledge the difference and resolve to try again the next day. This awareness itself will help us be more attentive the next day, opening opportunities to bring our everyday thoughts and actions into closer alignment with our goals.

The benefits of intention and dedication

Framing our days between intention setting and joyful dedication this way, even once a week, can change how we live. It's a purposeful approach of self-awareness, conscious intention, and focused effort—three precious gifts of contemplative practice—by which we take responsibility for our thoughts and actions and take charge of ourselves and our lives. As the Buddha put it, "You are your own enemy/and you are your own savior."[2] The Buddha saw that our thoughts, emotions, and actions are the primary sources of our suffering. Equally, our thoughts, emotions, and actions can be the source of our joy and freedom. Living, as much as possible, with conscious intention is the first step of this transformation. So, these two exercises in intention and dedication are the first step to greater clarity and cohesion in our life, our work, and our relationships with others.

Not only that, when our aspirations include the welfare and happiness of others, our deeds and our life as a whole acquire a purpose that is greater than our individual existence. On the global stage, perhaps the most compelling example of the power of an individual's conscious intention can be seen in the amazing story of South Africa's transition from apartheid to freedom. Nelson Mandela's commitment to nonviolence, racial harmony, and justice shaped his intention to create a different South Africa, is one historic example. It was a most inconvenient intention that found opposition in one form or another probably every day of his long life. Living true to such an intention doesn't happen without setting and resetting it, and drawing strength from dedicated reflection. Mandela's intention helped set the mood of the new nation. The result is a smooth and peaceful transition. A classical Buddhist text offers this metaphor: If a drop of water happens to fall into an ocean, some part of that water will remain, as long as that ocean remains; left on its own, that drop of water will just dry up.

A grandmother in her sixties who did the Stanford compassion training continued to work full-time, although she wanted to be with her grandchildren more. She felt that she would be letting her employer down by reducing her work hours, even though she was very much troubled by the fact that her grandchildren were growing up and she was not able to spend much time with them. Starting with intentions of compassion and kindness toward herself, she connected with her motivation to tell her boss that she wanted to reduce her hours. She says that her employer is happy, her grandchildren are happy, and she is happy. As she told her CCT instructor, she had always been someone who sacrificed for everyone else while not being true to some of her most deeply held values. This woman didn't just change the amount of time she spent with her grandchildren; she changed the way she lived her life.[3]

In my own life, intention has helped in so many areas. When my wife and I became parents, our conscious approach to parenting allowed us to shape with the values we cherish our interactions with our children when they were small. What mattered most to us was giving our love, trust, respect, and attention to our children in an atmosphere of warmth and intimacy. Everything else was details. As our daughters grew up and developed their own personalities, we brought into our intention specific thoughts about the style and quality of parenting we wanted to see from ourselves. For example: *May I respect my daughters as individuals in their own right rather than viewing them as extensions of my ego.* This said, we also wanted to be clear about boundaries. We recognized that routines are particularly important for small children, and when it came to school, for example, there would be no negotiation. Unless you're ill, you cannot miss school just because you don't feel like it. Yet, we didn't want to fall into nagging, either. So, for another example: *May I choose my fights wisely.*

Of course, occasionally we did and still do fall short on the intentions we set for ourselves. One of the things I discovered about myself through parenting—with some horror, I must admit—is how mad I could actually get. Rarely have I felt such intense frustration, especially with my younger daughter, Tara, when she was around three years old. Thanks to my habit of setting intentions, and the power of intentions to increase awareness and influence behavior, I would catch myself before I turned emotions into unskillful actions. Often I discovered that my own issues were the real triggers. Truly, small children give us precious lessons on our own selves. (Thank you, Tara!)

Intentions can help us with self-control, which can make our whole life feel so much less out of control. I remember when I first had, at Cambridge University in 1989, a laptop with a ten-megabyte hard disk on it. (This was a big deal then.) It came preloaded with games, including chess. The chess program allowed me to withdraw my last move when I played against the computer, which meant that I could get a preview of how the computer might respond to my move. Often in the evening, I would find myself playing chess without noticing how many hours had passed, cheating and taking back my move and changing it! Once I recognized how addictive this behavior was, I deleted the games from my computer, a discipline I adopted for my next laptop as well. By my third computer, I no longer had to delete the games.

My relationship with the Internet and e-mail today is shaped by that early intentional practice. As they have become ubiquitous, I have been proactive about containing their presence in my life. With e-mails, in particular, I have maintained a fairly strict discipline for nearly two decades now. I start my workday not with e-mails, but with at least an hour or two of actual work. When I then get to my e-mails, messages that I can reply to in less than a minute or two I take care of immediately or later that day. Those that require longer responses and some further reflection I defer for at least a day or two. And if I receive an e-mail on Friday, unless it is absolutely urgent, I wait until Monday to reply. I avoid touching e-mail after work, as well as during the weekend, except when I am on the road. The benefits are obvious to me: space and time to be more fully present with my family, or with myself. It's the conscious intention to be fully present, as much as possible, that helps maintain this discipline.

For most young people, including my two teenage daughters, who use digital space as part of their everyday world, my relationship with the digital world will seem parochial, to say the least. Still, whatever shape it takes, the fact remains that we can all benefit from a conscious, proactive approach to this dimension of our life today.

I am quite sure that there is a link between today's high volume of electronic mail and pervasive feelings of being overwhelmed and stressed out. Conscious intention, applied to this or any other stressor in our lives, works as a buffer against these negative feelings of stress. For one thing—and this was true for me with both chess and parenting—it's a way of asserting control where you can, and so much of stress comes from feeling like our lives are out of our control. When we set an intention in the morning, we're making a choice about what kind of day we want to have. We're taking life into our own hands instead of waiting for it to happen to us. We may waver or forget our intention completely for stretches of the day, but the very act of setting—and resetting, and *re*-resetting—an intention acknowledges that we have a choice, and that in itself can give us a sense of control. For another thing, setting an intention is a form of preparation. We study for exams or prepare talking points and rehearse for presentations, for example, because most of us would find it unbearably stressful to show up unprepared. In the process of preparing, we consider various possible scenarios, which protects us to some degree from being caught off guard. It helps to come prepared for the day, just like any other activity we care about.

> *May all beings attain happiness and its causes.*
> *May all beings be free from suffering and its causes.*
> *May all beings never be separated from joy that is free of*
> * misery.*
> *May all beings abide in equanimity, free from bias of*
> * attachment and aversion.*

How intention becomes motivation

It matters that we set an intention, and it matters what intention we set. However, as anyone who has ever tried to keep a New Year's resolution knows, setting an intention, even a really sincere, good intention, is by no means a fait accompli. We may wish to be compassionate and caring toward others, and say this to ourselves in the morning, yet find ourselves that very afternoon—or much sooner—in a rather more self-interested, judgmental place. The relationship between our conscious intentions on the one hand and the often not-so-conscious motivations that drive our thoughts and actions on the other is complex. But with persistent awareness and reflection, we can, over time, bring our motivations more into line with our intentions.

The Dalai Lama once suggested a simple way of checking our motivations, by posing these questions to ourselves:

- Is it just for me or for others?

- For the benefit of the few or for the many?

- For now or for the future?[4]

These questions help clarify our motivations by bringing critical self-awareness (critical in the sense of objective and discerning, not judgmental) to our relationship with what we do. They also help remind us to bring compassion to bear upon our thoughts and actions. We can ask these questions before we do something, while we're doing it, or after we have done it—there will always be another opportunity to (re)set our intention and another chance to act in accordance with that intention.

Two American experts in caregiving behavior, Jennifer Crocker and Amy Canevello, distinguish between what they evocatively call *egosystem* and *ecosystem* motivations.[5] With egosystem motivations, they explain, caregiving is a means to satisfy the caregiver's needs and desires. In an egosystem, satisfaction is a zero-sum game: Caregivers compete for, say, status and praise for being good at what they do. In contrast, caregiving in an ecosystem is motivated by genuine concern for the well-being of others. Although ecosystem caregiving might result in benefits for the caregiver—providing a sense of purpose and joy, for example—these benefits are not the primary reasons why people provide care. They are, as we saw in Chapter 1, unintended benefits of kindness. Ecosystem caregiving tends to be more cooperative, because caregivers with compassionate goals define success in terms of what's helpful for others.[6] On the emotional level as well, ecosystem caregivers feel more peaceful, clear-minded, and loving.

This said, Crocker and Canevello admit that there is a complex interrelation between the two systems. Our motivations are often mixed, and our motivations and intentions can even be contradictory. If I shout at my teenage daughter for coming home late, my intention is to help her take responsibility for her action, to remind her that people depend on her, and that there are consequences for breaking trust. The motivation, on the other hand, could be that I was afraid for her safety at night and wanted her to feel as scared as I was. Or it could be, selfishly, that I felt slighted by what I saw as defiance, and wanted to reassert my power. It could be that I was angry and it felt good, in the moment, to yell. Moreover, motivations can fluctuate from moment to moment in a single individual. What the contemplative practice of intention setting suggests is this: With practice, we can learn to tap into our ecosystem motivations, rather than get stuck in our egosystem. The rewards of acting according to our best intentions, when we experience them, reflect on them, and take joy in them, redirect our motivations from one system to the other. With practice, our intentions will take on the force of habit, and even our neural networks will "realign" to get behind our intentions.

The question of how we motivate ourselves to pursue our

deeper aspirations has been a major interest in the long history of Buddhist psychology.[7] In Buddhist thinking, motivation is a matter of desire, more specifically the *desire to act* accompanied with a sense of *purpose*. Say, in the case of being more compassionate, it's by making an emotional connection with compassion and its objectives that we arouse in ourselves the desire to act compassionately. And it's through seeing the benefits that we acquire a sense of purpose in being more compassionate.

Contemporary psychology has only relatively recently come to appreciate the role of emotions in motivating our behavior. For a long time, the Western theory of action was dominated by rational choice theory, and emotions were accused of clouding the process rather than being an integral part of the system. To articulate the dual dimension of our motivation—cognitive awareness of and emotional connection with our goals—Buddhist psychology uses a term that is almost impossible to capture in any single word in English. The Sanskrit term *shraddha* (*depa* in Tibetan) has a broad range of meaning, the important ones being "faith," "trust," "belief," or "confidence," connoting "appreciation" and "admiration" as well. *Shraddha* is a felt sense like trust, rather than a cognitive state like belief or knowledge. Experientially, *shraddha* feels something like attachment or attraction to our goal, like being inspired to play guitar when you see a rock star do it. It's this quality, *shraddha*, that primes our heart and mind to roll up our sleeves and play.

How do we tap our emotional reservoir? Cognitions play a critical role, which the early Buddhist texts characterize as *seeing* the value of doing something. Not unlike what today's corporations do when they advertise their consumer products, often Buddhist texts would begin by extolling the virtues of a given ideal or pursuit that the author wished to advocate. Through cognitive engagement, such as seeing the benefits, we connect intention with motivation. So, within this causal nexus, the crucial link to watch for is the one between our awareness of the goal and why we would go for it, our feelings about the goal, and our desire or will to pursue it.

Then, again, it's the joy we take in our efforts (the courage to try, the dedication to stick with it) and their results (the camaraderie of playing together, in the case of learning guitar; the magic of making music) that helps sustain our motivations over the long run. Or, in other words, makes us want to keep trying and keep doing it. Parents who have struggled with their child taking up a new instrument will recognize how everything changes the moment the child begins enjoying it. This is called *intrinsic* motivation, as opposed to the *extrinsic* motivation of, for example, the parent rewarding the child with more screen time for practicing her instrument. From decades of motivation research, we know that intrinsic motivation is far more stable and enduring.[8] The process of setting intentions and joyfully reflecting on them in dedication is how, over time, we transform extrinsic into intrinsic motivations, and thereby sustain the energy and purpose to live true to our best aspirations.

> *May all beings attain happiness and its causes.*
> *May all beings be free from suffering and its causes.*
> *May all beings never be separated from joy that is free of*
> *   misery.*
> *May all beings abide in equanimity, free from bias of*
> *   attachment and aversion.*

5

Making Way for Compassion
How Focused Awareness Keeps Us on Track

We let ourselves be at the mercy of our thoughts and our thoughts at the mercy of our negative emotions, in this way we undermine ourselves.

—Tibetan saying

Choice of attention—to pay attention to this or ignore that— is to the inner life what choice is to the outer life.

—W. H. Auden (1907–1973)

As the next step in our training, we cultivate three skills we will use to apply our mind to compassion. First, we learn to *quiet the mind.* Then we develop *concentration* through focused attention. And we strengthen our *awareness*, a relaxed, open state in which we can observe our thoughts, feelings, and behavior as they arise, without being overtaken by them. (Awareness is, in fact, the most important "active ingredient" of modern mindfulness practice.) Together, these three skills are so useful that we repeat them at the start of each successive step of the course. We call them, collectively, Settling the Mind. In the process of settling the mind, we develop equanimity, a calm, grounded, open mind that has room to hold all of our experiences, including our own and others' need and pain.

We don't need to develop these skills to feel compassion for someone. As we have seen, that may happen quite naturally and spontaneously. But we do need these skills if we don't want to leave it up to chance. In some cases, especially when it comes to ourselves, as we have also seen, we find that we are not able to respond with compassion and kindness even though we wish we would. In Chapter 3, we considered more than a few reasons why resistance may get in our way. Resistance, negative judgment, and self-involvement all can hijack our attention and reactions. Our quiet, concentration, and awareness skills help us guide our mind the way we would like it to go.

Mind wandering: A default state of our brain?

A recent and memorable study by two psychologists at Harvard University, Matthew A. Killingsworth and Daniel T. Gilbert, powerfully demonstrated two basic facts of our everyday mind also recognized in Buddhist psychology:[1] Our default state of mind is that of wandering, and this mind wandering is a source of unhappiness. In order to obtain real-life data, instead of conducting the experiment in a lab the researchers used a method known as *experience sampling*, in this case with an iPhone app they developed called Track Your Happiness. In an initial study on 2,250 volunteers, the Web-based app would ping the subjects at random intervals, asking them what they were doing at that moment, how happy they were, and whether they were thinking about their current activity or something else; and if they were thinking about something else, whether they were thinking about something pleasant, unpleasant, or neutral. Participants chose from a list of twenty-two activities they might be doing, including working, walking, eating, resting or sleeping, shopping, commuting, watching television, and "nothing special."

Almost half the time, people reported that their minds were wandering, and this was true at least 30 percent of the time in every activity on the list except making love.[2] (One has to commend the dedication of these subjects, responding even when they were making love! I hope they warned their partners that this might happen.) The researchers found that when people were mind wandering, they reported feeling happy only 56 percent of the time, in contrast to 66 percent of the time when they were paying attention to their present-moment activity. (The findings do not say anything about the causal direction: Were people happy because they were focused, or were they focused because they were happy?) In their published results, the researchers suggest that mind wandering appears to be the human brain's default mode of operation and conclude, "A human mind is a wandering mind, and a wandering mind is an unhappy mind ... The ability to think about what is not happening is a cognitive achievement that comes at an emotional cost." Since that seminal article in the journal *Science* in 2010, Killingsworth has repeated the experiment with many more thousands of subjects and in more than eighty countries across the world, all of which seem to support the initial findings.

It turns out, not surprisingly, not everything about mind

wandering is bad. Even Killingsworth and Gilbert's study revealed that it is *not* associated with unhappiness 44 percent of the time. Subsequent studies have found that mind wandering plays an important role in our mental life. For one thing, our mind's ability to wander is what lets us think about more than one thing at a time—multi-tasking, if you want—a facility that seems to be associated with working (immediate short-term) memory. People with greater-capacity working memories are able to retain more information at any given time, an ability that has been linked to intelligence, such as IQ and reading comprehension. Second, a study of mind wandering using neuroimaging techniques found that it's involved in the formation and consolidation of memory.[3] Finally, mind wandering is important for creativity, something most artists know from experience.[4] In popular convention too, at least in the West, we recognize that creative insight often appears when we least expect it, when we are not trying to force it and our mind is open and free. Science seems to agree that we get our best ideas in the shower.

The toxic part of mind wandering may have more to do with its self-referentiality than, as many have suggested, with not being in the present moment. A disproportionate number of the thoughts in a wandering mind seem to be about "I," "me," and "mine." A cluster of specific brain regions implicated in self-referential thinking is strongly involved in mind wandering as well. And when our sense of self is involved, we tend to relate to others and the world around us with greater emotional and personal bias.[5] In plain English, when we're thinking about ourselves, we tend to think we're more important than we are, and feel there's more at stake than there actually is. So, much of our unhappiness associated with mind wandering may have to do with *where* our minds wander to, and the contrast we experience between the way things actually are (the world doesn't revolve around us, we're not supposed to be perfectly comfortable all the time or live forever, et cetera) and the way we think they are supposed to be (what about me? Look at me! Why me?).

Here's where settling the mind comes in: We need those three skills to stop being unwitting victims of our wandering minds. We need some peace and quiet—not a weekend in the country, necessarily, but the everyday ability to quiet and still the mind so that we can be free, at least for a chosen period of time, from the restless energy of thoughts and emotions that usually storm through it. We also need cognitive skills to intervene in our own thinking. We need to have focus in order to shift our attention from ourselves to others and the world around us. And we need some ability to pay attention to what the mind is doing so that we are not always at the mercy of its automatic habits. We cultivate these skills through contemplative practices.

Quieting the mind

When we are sick and our doctor tells us that we need to rest, we know how to do this physically. We slow down, do less, and if necessary even lie in bed. But mind rest doesn't come so easily for most of us. Usually, we rely on distraction and use one kind of activity to divert our mind from another more stressful, tiring one, especially from work. We watch TV, read a book, go on holiday, or have a drink—anything for a break from our everyday routine. But that's still doing something, and it still leaves us dependent on these other things. (What happens if there is a power-cut? If someone interrupts our reading? If we don't happen to be on holiday? You get the idea.) Contemplative practice takes a different approach, giving us a way to quiet our mind from within—not by running away from it, but by approaching it; not by distracting it, but by applying it; and not by fueling the fire with more external stimuli, but by diffusing its restless energy and letting the fires go out.

This is, however, not easy. A recent study, involving seven hundred people in eleven different experiments, showed that many of us would go to great lengths to avoid being alone with our thoughts.[6] In the study, most of the participants were uncomfortable being alone with nothing to do even for less than fifteen minutes; some preferred administering electric shocks to themselves rather than introspection. One theory is that when we're alone, we tend to dwell on what is wrong with our lives, and this, naturally, makes us feel unhappy. Contemplative practice teaches us how to be with our thoughts courageously and attentively, yet free ourselves from the negative side effects of thinking.

To quiet the mind, we learn to slow it down to stillness. Classical Buddhist texts use the analogy of choppy, turbid water to illustrate the character of a restless mind. Still the water, and gradually the silts and other impurities will settle, revealing the water's clear character. Similarly, if we can still the mind and let it stand unperturbed by our usual squalls of thinking—anticipation, apprehension, and judgment—we will be able to see the truth of things more clearly, what really matters, what serves our purpose, and what we need to do.

Here are two contemplative exercises to help you quiet the mind, drawn from the Tibetan tradition but adapted for secular use. The first one is a deep-breathing exercise; the second is a kind of mind-expanding exercise, because the more spacious our minds are, the more room there is for all of our experience, and for us to step back from what's happening there, so we are not just caught up in it. The point is not to stop our thoughts or feelings from arising—this would be impossible. The point is to learn to be with them, with enough awareness that we can watch them go by. With more space comes more perspective: We can *have* thoughts, and see them for what they are, rather than *be* our thoughts.

If you are doing contemplative exercises for the first time, you could spend around five minutes on the two exercises together in a single sitting. Start with the breathing practice, using two-thirds of your sitting for this, and conclude with the spaciousness exercise. If possible, repeat these several times during the day.

EXERCISE: Deep Breathing

Choose a convenient time of the day, when you are unlikely to be disturbed, at least for few minutes. If you are new to meditation, it's also helpful to find a place—a quiet room, a corner, a special cushion—that you can associate with your practice. This way when you sit there, the physical setting itself will cue you and help create the right ambience.

Adopt a physical posture that is comfortable. You could sit on a chair, on a cushion on the floor with your legs crossed, or if you prefer, lie on your back on the floor (though this will make it harder for people prone to sleepiness). If you're on a cushion or a chair, unless you have health problems try to keep your back straight, free from the backrest or wall behind you. Let your eyes relax. You can either keep them gently closed or gaze softly in front of you at an angle where, if you were to look, you would see the tip of your nose. Personally, I prefer to have my eyes closed in a relaxed manner. You can place your hands gently on your thighs with the tips of your fingers resting on your knees. Alternatively, you could rest your hands on your lap, with the back of the right hand resting on the left palm and your two thumbs lightly touching each other, forming a sort of triangle. The point is to choose a hand position that is relaxed and will not cause any strain when you keep it for a period of time.

Now begin by expanding your chest so that your lungs open wide. Then take deep, diaphragmatic breaths, each time breathing all the way down into your belly as if you are filling up the torso with the in-breath from the bottom to the top. Just like when you pour water into a jug, it fills up from the bottom. Breathe deeply in this way, one breath at a time, and feel your belly rising each time as the air fills it. When you exhale, let your breath out at a slow, measured pace. If you find it's more relaxing to let the breath out from your mouth, do so.

Inhale slowly, deeply, and attentively enough that you can actually hear the sound of the air coming in through your nostrils. Then retain the breath for two to three seconds, and let it out, again in a measured, longish exhale. Breathe in ... retain ... and now breathe out, "hah." Do this again:

Breathe in ... keep it ... and breathe out ... Repeat five to ten times.

In most cases, simply breathing in this deliberate, measured way will bring your mind back from wandering, back into your body and its immediate experience of breathing. This said, if you need further props to help bring your mind into your body, then as you breathe in, you can mentally note "in" ... and hold a pause, and as you breathe out, mentally note "out." Also, if it helps, you can pay attention to your chest expanding and contracting as you breathe in and out, or to your belly rising and falling.

Another variation you can use, especially if you happen to be feeling particularly stressed or agitated, is to imagine, as you inhale deeply, the cool air coming in through your lungs, spreading to the areas in your body where you feel tense, and relaxing them as the breath spreads through them. The neck, shoulders, upper or lower back, and abdomen are common areas of tension. Then, as you breathe out, imagine releasing the tension, tightness, and stress along with the warm breath that goes out. Imagine, as a result, you feel light, flexible, and free in your body.

* * *

Once you get used to this simple deep-breathing exercise, you can use it to invoke calmness wherever and whenever you need. You could do this at the start of your workday, at your desk at the office. You could do this on an airplane if you're feeling afraid—when there is turbulence, for instance. I never used to be afraid of flying, but several years ago, on my way back from Edmonton to Montreal, the plane hit an air pocket and dropped suddenly, without any warning from the pilot. After that, every time I flew and there was more than a little turbulence, my body would tense up in fear, even though my conscious mind said everything was fine. It took at least a year before I got over this fear completely. Deep breathing helped a lot.

I also use this exercise to down-regulate anytime I find myself feeling agitated. So, although deep breathing is considered a preliminary practice in the Buddhist contemplative tradition—to help settle the mind before applying it to more specific objectives—the effects go way beyond its traditional role.

EXERCISE: Spacious Mind

This next, short exercise complements the deep-breathing exercise well. Here we evoke a sense of spaciousness or expansiveness, which helps the mind calm down, since so much of the tension and restlessness in the mind arises from feelings of constriction, rigidity, and heaviness. The spacious mind feels like the view from the top of a mountain. In Shimla, in northern India where I grew up, there were roofed resting points called *hava khana* (literally meaning "house of air") on viewpoints along the road. I used to love sitting quietly on the bench in these houses of air. Looking at a photograph of such a vista may give you the same feeling. Or you could lie on your back on a clear day and gaze into the deep blue sky above and feel its spaciousness. When you have an experiential sense of spaciousness, it becomes easier to invoke similar states in a sitting.

For this exercise, once you have done some deep breathing, proceed:

Adopt a comfortable breathing rhythm that doesn't require conscious effort to maintain, a pace your breath would naturally find when you're in a relaxed state of mind.

Once you have settled on your breath, imagine your mind is a wide-open space, vast, expansive, and boundless. Think of your thoughts, feelings, hopes, and fears as clouds that form and disappear into this vast open space. Whatever thoughts arise ("I wish I was calmer," "He said this and that," "I mustn't forget to do x, y, and z," and so on) or whatever emotions ("I'm feeling restless ... hurt ... confused ... "), see that they're as insubstantial as clouds. Imagine they arise one by one and disappear into the limitless expanse of your mind. Then rest your mind in this spaciousness for a while, feeling calm and relaxed—at least imagine feeling so. Stay silent in this way for one to two minutes.

* * *

For some people, chanting or listening to chants might help to quiet the mind. Chanting was part of my daily life as a monk for a long time, and some of those times, chanting with my fellow monks, were among the most profoundly quiet my mind has ever been. In those moments, I felt as if time itself—for that matter the world too—stood still, and there was only the sound and cadence of the chant. But chanting is not for everyone. Breathing, on the other hand, is.

Focusing the mind

In addition to a relatively quiet mind, compassion requires some ability to apply our mind in a focused way—in other words, concentration: consciously, deliberately paying attention to something and sustaining that attention, at least for a little while. Anyone who has watched a dog spy a squirrel in a park, or nature programs on television, will know what it means to focus with single-pointed attention. Most of us will also know from experience what it feels like to be totally focused, when we're gripped by a powerful film, deep into a book, or immersed in conversation with a friend. As committed as I am to formal sitting practice, I have experienced some of my deepest states of absorption away from the meditation cushion, in the midst of crowds and activity. As a young monk in southern India, I used to love reading, in addition to Jane Austen, thick novels, my favorites being those of Dostoyevsky, Tolstoy, James A. Michener, and James Clavell. Waiting for my bus, I could easily pass several hours quite happily reading, while a chaotic scene unfolded around me of people rushing, peddlers shouting in singsong voices, and the noise and fumes that are typical of crowded Indian bus stations.

In everyday settings like these, we may happen to experience concentrated states in response to factors outside our conscious control, such as environment and time, as well as the kind of mood we happen to be in. Through contemplative training, we learn to harness our natural capacity to apply our mind, so that we may choose when and what to focus on.

In the following section I describe two different attention

exercises. For both of these, it's helpful to quiet the mind first through the deep-breathing practice. The aim of these trainings is not some kind of superhuman, laser-sharp focus maintained unwaveringly for hours at a time. Rather, it is to help us develop some ability to focus our attention, apply our mind, and sustain that attention for at least a few minutes at a time.

EXERCISE: Focused Attention Through Mindful Breathing

Once you have taken three to five deep, diaphragmatic breaths in the manner described in the deep-breathing exercise, and have released any tension you found in your body, continue as follows:

Choose a pace of breathing that is not shallow but also not forced. To help anchor your awareness of the sensation of your breathing, choose a focal point, such as the tips of your nostrils, where you feel subtle sensations as you breathe in and out, or your belly, where you feel the sensation of its rising and falling as you breathe. This way, whenever you notice that your mind has wandered, you can bring your attention back by returning to this focal point.

When you have found a comfortable rhythm, start mentally counting your breaths, with each round of an inhalation and exhalation as one cycle. Breathe in . . . and as you breathe out, mentally say "one." Breathe in . . . breathe out, "two." Breathe in . . . breathe out, "three," and so on.

Initially, you could count up to five or ten, restart the count from one, and repeat this process several times, for five to ten minutes. If you lose count, do not beat yourself up; simply note it, gently bring your attention back to your breath, and start the count again.

As you get used to the exercise, say, after a few weeks of practice, you can increase your count up to twenty or thirty, and repeat. Maybe by then you could even increase the length of your sitting to ten or fifteen minutes.

Once you get good at counting serially—that is, with no lapses in attention—you could make it more challenging by counting from both directions: Start by counting up, say from one to ten, and then count backward from ten, and repeat this counting, as before, for up to five minutes at a time during your sitting.

* * *

Counting our breath as a means to focus our mind is an efficient technique, especially for beginners. Because we are giving our mind something to do rather than simply turning inward, counting breaths makes it easier for us to sustain our attention.

ALTERNATIVE EXERCISE

As an alternative to counting, you could try this variation. Here, in place of counting your breaths, we note the cycles of in-breath and out-breath. For this too, begin with some deep breathing to calm your mind.

Then, breathe comfortably, mentally noting your in-breaths

and out-breaths: As you breathe in, note "in," and as you breathe out, note "out." Do this for five to ten minutes.

* * *

Once you have gained some confidence in breath counting (or noting)—say, you are able to count twenty or thirty breaths at a time without losing your attention; or, noting in-breaths and out-breaths, to maintain your attention on the movements of your breath for thirty seconds at a time, you could then add the next step of mindful breathing practice:

ADVANCED EXERCISE

Concentrate your attention on the focal point you have chosen—the tips of your nostrils or your belly—and simply observe as you breathe in and breathe out. Refrain from counting or mentally labeling the in-breaths and out-breaths. Simply let your mind rest on your breath and observe; be aware of the sensation of breathing. Do nothing; just follow your breath as you breathe in and out. Whenever you lose your focus and find that your mind has been distracted, gently bring it back to your focal point and let it rest on your breath again.

* * *

During the sitting, your mind will wander, straying from your chosen object of focus. At the beginning, you might not even notice when you become distracted. If this happens, don't be discouraged; it is quite normal (remember, "a human mind is a wandering mind"). Maintaining your focus undistracted for more than a few seconds at a time can be hard. In fact, part of the learning curve is to see how quickly you catch yourself drifting away from your chosen object, and how kindly you can bring yourself back.

When you first start doing the focused attention exercises, keep your sessions short. Even when you do a short sitting (say, five minutes), it's helpful to take short breaks in between stretches of concentration. Quite often, people in their initial enthusiasm insist on long sittings. They assume that short sittings will have no real impact, but this is not true. For mental training, regularity is more important, especially when you're first learning. Also, keeping your sessions short increases your chances of enjoying the exercise. Tibetan meditation masters often emphasize the benefits of ending your sitting on a positive note, with a sense of joy rather than frustration or fatigue.

Once you have done regular practice for a few months, however, consider doing an intensive retreat, where you can spend a few days doing nothing but meditation. The isolation of the retreat setting, maintaining silence, the regimen of regular long sittings, all of this contributes to an environment conducive to slowing down and just being with your mind. Such a retreat experience can help deepen your practice and put you more at ease with your mind.

Note that I have described the three variations of mindful breathing so far in order of difficulty: The first is easiest for most people; the second, a bit harder; and the third, hardest of all. In the first two exercises we give our mind something active to do, counting breaths or mentally noting the activity of breathing in and out. This active engagement helps us to gather our mind, direct our attention to our breath, and sustain that attention. That's why the third exercise, in which we simply rest our awareness on the sensation of breathing, is the most challenging of the three. We haven't given the mind an assignment beyond being there.

In the traditional meditation manuals, these three breathing exercises are sometimes presented as distinct practices suited to different individuals, but I personally find it more helpful to view the first two as alternate exercises, with the third as a more advanced stage of mindful breathing. In my daily practice, I still do a few rounds of breath counting, skip the mental noting exercise, and then focus mainly on the third breath awareness exercise. It's a gentle way of channeling my attention progressively inward, with less dependence on giving my mind something active to do. In the end, each of us needs to see for ourself what works best—a combination of two or all three, or sticking with just one. Whatever you choose, the key is to do it regularly.

EXERCISE: Focused Attention Using an Image

You can also focus your attention with the help of an image. This is particularly appropriate if you come from a religious tradition that includes objects of special significance. For a Buddhist, for example, it could be an image of a serene Buddha; for a Christian, it could be the cross, and so on. In the secular context, you could choose any object that has special resonance for you—a painting that you feel drawn to, a beautiful artifact, a candle in front of you. It doesn't have to be anything fancy. Traditional meditation manuals suggest neutral objects as well—it could be a pebble. Or, you could use an internal image, such as an orb of light at your heart or at your forehead.

Say you have chosen a candle as your object of focus; the exercise would look like this:

Light a candle and place it about three feet in front of you, ideally at eye level.

Proceed, as before, with three to five deep, diaphragmatic breaths, including, if necessary, breathing into and releasing any tension and tightness you may be feeling in your body.

Once you have brought your mind inward a little and settled it this way, the focused attention training begins. Gaze at the candlelight as steadily as you can, trying not to give in to any urge to conceptualize what you see—"It's quite bright," "It's not flickering," "It's beautiful," and so on. Simply rest your awareness in the bare perception of this candle flame, with a sense of abandon. Keep your gaze soft, not forcing your eyes to look in a particular way.

As you stay in this experience of pure gazing, gradually you will get a sense of the candle in your mind's eye. Like a portrait shot with a good camera, the image sits before you in the foreground, with its background blurred. As your attention homes in on its object, there will be just the image of the candle in front of you. At that point, as far as your experience is concerned, the rest of the world has ceased to exist. It is just a blur. Stay in this state for a little while, with only the candlelight in focus.

When the vibrancy of this experience wanes and your mind starts to slacken, take a break by opening your eyes widely and looking around. Then return your gaze to the candle and repeat the process, as before.

* * *

If you like the image-based attention practice and want to use it as your main approach, here is how you can create your own program. Begin the sitting with three to five deep breaths to quiet and relax your mind, followed by one to two minutes of breath counting or noting. For the rest of the sitting, practice focusing on your chosen image, as previously described.

I began attention training as a young monk, not through the kind of contemplative exercises I've just described, but through daily memorization that was part of my monastic education. Most of the texts I had to memorize were beyond the comprehension of a young adolescent, so I found them quite boring, to say the least. Yet, memorize them I did. Fortunately, almost all of the texts were in verse, and their metered lines made for somewhat easier chanting and memorization.

The best time to memorize is early morning, and during the day I would rehearse what I had memorized several times to keep it fresh. In the evening, I had to recite it to a senior monk. Then, before going to bed, I would recite to myself the entire text I had memorized so far, from the beginning to the point where I happened to be, chanting it outside in the dark. Once I had completed one text, I would chant the whole thing every night for at least a month. In this way, I would progressively consolidate the memory from temporary to long-term. This is an amazing system. Today, after more than thirty years, I can still chant many of these texts from memory, so long as I reread them once or twice as a refresher!

I am aware that memorization has a bad reputation in modern education, especially in the West, as a kind of rote learning. However, it can be a powerful approach to attention training, especially for young children. There is something to be said for bringing it back into education, not as a substitute for learning, but as a means of training attention and memory.

Strengthening meta-awareness

Our third mind-settling skill, after quieting and focusing, is the ability to have a greater degree of awareness, whether it's in relation to our own thoughts, feelings, and actions, or with respect to what is happening around us. Both Buddhist and contemporary psychology refer to the type of awareness that concerns us here as "meta-cognitive awareness" or "meta-awareness." *Meta-* is a prefix, from the Greek, meaning "beyond," as in *metaphysics*—literally, "beyond physics." In contemporary English, however, we use *meta-* to mean a larger framework within which we can speak about a particular phenomenon. For example, *metadata* is data about data, and *metacognition* is cognition of cognition, or thinking about thinking.

For our training purposes, we're interested in the cognitive process by which we bring awareness to the dynamics of our thoughts, emotions, and behavior. Instead of constantly being swept away by the tides of whatever is happening in our life, we learn to step back and observe the theater of our mind as if we were not a participant but an objective spectator. It's this dimension of perspective, of observing from a vantage point with a little distance, that makes this particular type of awareness very different from ordinary awareness. This skill of simply being present and observing our body, feelings, mind, and its contents, without judgment or resistance, is really the core of modern mindfulness practice. This exercise is adapted from Buddhist meditation, and involves attentiveness with no specific focal point as an object.

EXERCISE: Meta-Awareness

Here again, begin your sitting with three to five deep, diaphragmatic breaths and breathe through any tension and tightness in your body.

To further quiet your mind, you could also do some breath counting, followed by simple breath awareness, for a minute or two.

Once you feel settled, release your mind from its focus on the breath and let it rest with awareness. If you keep your eyes closed for this exercise, you have one fewer sensory modalities to worry about. However, if you wish to keep them open, it's helpful to face a plain wall (without colors, patterns, or pictures to distract you).

Now, while staying in present-moment awareness, notice whatever might happen to enter, exit, or pass by your awareness—a sound of a vehicle on the road outside, birds singing or crickets chirping somewhere, the beginning of an ache in your knees, a thought or a memory, and so on. Staying alert in your awareness, simply observe whatever comes, without trying to suppress it, and without adding fuel to it, either. Just observe, acknowledge, and let go ... observe, acknowledge, and let go...

You could do this simple awareness practice for up to ten minutes. If it's helpful, especially in the initial stage, do it in successive chunks with fifteen- to twenty-second breaks in between.

* * *

Walking meditation, which is popular today in the modern meditation movement, is another form of awareness training. You could do this by walking very slowly, in a measured way, in stages:

EXERCISE: Walking Meditation

Find a quiet spot, either outside or indoors, where there is enough space to take at least five to ten steps without bumping into something. Stand, and keep your body relaxed, with your hands either in front of you, the two palms together, or keep your hands loose, with your arms hanging straight on either side of your body. Keep your eyes open, softly gazing down in front of you. If you are doing this practice indoors, or outdoors with weather and other factors permitting, you might want to walk barefoot to feel the contact when your feet touch the ground.

Once you have your body posture settled, start walking. Lifting your right leg with awareness, as in slow motion, mentally say, "Now I am lifting my right foot." As you place your right foot on the ground, think, "Now I am placing it on the ground." Then, as you lean forward and slowly lift your left leg, think, "Now I am lifting my left foot," and finally, as you place it on the ground, think, "Now I am placing my left foot on the ground." Repeat the process and do this walking meditation for several minutes, up to ten minutes at a time.

* * *

You can do walking meditation at a normal speed too. Because of the faster pace, obviously, you will not have time to break down the walk into four distinct stages and mentally note each of these. Nonetheless, you can be mindful of lifting the right foot, placing it to the ground, lifting the left foot, placing it to the ground, and so on. In this way, you maintain a simple awareness of the act of walking. Actually, what we today call walking meditation is, in traditional Buddhist contexts, a part of "post-sitting practices," the idea being that the monks bring full awareness to their everyday activities, such as walking, and not only when they're sitting meditating.

If you can use your normal walking as walking meditation, you are more likely to make meditation part of your daily activity. I walk my dog, Tsomo, a Tibetan terrier, every day after lunch for about half an hour, and I use part of that walk for meditation. So, for instance, if you are walking in the park, you can begin by counting a few breaths (for this, you might want to slow down or even pause for a moment and sit on a bench). Then begin simple awareness of walking—now lifting the right foot, placing it on the ground, now lifting the left foot ... After a few minutes, let go of your attention from the walk and maintain simple awareness with no particular focus. Whatever happens to pass your awareness, external (sounds of traffic outside the park, the sight of people passing by) or internal (thoughts about people, feelings of aversion to traffic sounds, thoughts about something that happened two days ago), simply observe it and let it go. After a while, return to your awareness of walking, then go back to simple awareness, and so on. In this way, alternate between these two phases of awareness.

To quiet the mind is to relax the mind. We learn to unhook our awareness from the restless, tiresome activity of habitual thought patterns and from our instinctive and automatic emotional reactions to these. We learn to quiet the ceaseless internal chatter of what-ifs, and we learn to let go of the over-interpreting, ruminating, and clinging to our experiences that we tend to do even when the experiences themselves have long gone. A quiet(er) mind is a place we can more readily be present, which makes us available to care for ourselves and others.

When we focus the mind, we rein in its natural tendency to wander, thus freeing up mental resources that would otherwise dissipate willy-nilly. More important, we learn to bring attention to what we truly value. Paying closer attention leads to greater awareness and understanding of our own and other people's experience—crucial for arousing our natural capacity for empathy. In fact, without attention, there is no empathy and understanding; and without these there is no compassion. It's as simple as this.

Finally, by strengthening our meta-awareness, we become more self-aware and more aware of others. We put ourselves in the courageous position of being with things as they actually are, since we know there's a calm place within ourselves where we can stand. We acknowledge our thoughts and feelings, including the more adverse and painful ones. As we saw in Chapter 3, because of our natural aversion to suffering, often we relate to our negative experience with denial and resistance. Not only does this cause further suffering for us; it also prevents us from connecting with other people's suffering. Meta-awareness lets us be with our own and others' suffering without feeling threatened by it, because we can step back and make room for all of it, rather than get caught up and thrown off. This, in turn, allows our compassionate instinct to express itself as it naturally does in the face of suffering and need, when it's not held back by fear.

6

Getting Unstuck

Escaping the Prison of Excessive Self-Involvement

There is no charm equal to tenderness of heart.

—Jane Austen (1775–1817)

If you temper your heart with loving-kindness and prepare it like a fertile soil, and then plant the seed of compassion, it will greatly flourish.

—Kamalashila (eighth century)

The English verb *to care*, with its multiple meanings, is interesting. When we say we care about something we are saying that we take it seriously. When we say we care about someone we are saying that we are interested in that person. Most important, when we say we care for someone we mean that we feel a sense of concern for that person's well-being. In English, we use the same word to refer to the act that flows from such feelings of concern and interest. So to say, "I am taking care of the children" is to say that I am looking after the needs of the children. These layered meanings of the word *care* capture, to my mind, an important logic of our heart: *If we attach importance to someone we will feel greater concern for the person, and as a result, we will also show greater interest in his or her well-being.* This is why paying attention, from the previous chapter, is an indispensable link in the experience—and ultimately action— of caring for someone.

So far, the chain looks like this:

intention ➡ motivation ➡ attention ➡ loving-kindness and compassion ➡ acts of kindness

This chapter is about the loving-kindness and compassion link. In Buddhist compassion meditation, we practice raising feelings of affection and concern for someone we care about. We start with people we already care about, and once we have a feel for it, we practice caring about more and more people, and ultimately about all living beings, until love and compassion become our basic orientation toward everyone. A tangible benefit of this practice is that our hearts open. We reach outside ourselves, and life can reach in and touch us, and this is what it means to be human. Ancient Buddhist texts speak of something called *anukampa*,[1] meaning the feeling of "caring for" or "caring after," a term translated by some as "trembling of the heart," evoking the image of a heart that trembles or vibrates with sensitivity and aliveness—a heart literally moved by caring. Most of us know what a trembling heart feels like. Attending to people's needs, including our own, is what moves our hearts and makes us feel alive in the fullest sense. The more we care, the more we will be able to bring this heart energy to bear on the situation at hand.

Opening your heart in everyday life

For a long time in the West, at least back to Aristotle, we have defined our humanness primarily in rational terms. More recently, we've come to recognize that we are also emotional beings, with aesthetic and spiritual sensibilities. For me, a life without feeling touched, inspired, and moved by caring would be a shadow of a human life. We feel most alive when we are touched and moved by other people and the world around us, when we feel connected with others, when we find meaning and purpose—in other words, when we care about something other and greater than ourselves. Caring in this way makes us human; it's what keeps us going. To use a well-worn metaphor, we are hardwired to connect.

However, caring presupposes receptivity, an openness on our part to being touched. Even to fall in love, we need to be receptive; we need to be susceptible to being affected by another person. We cannot will ourselves to fall in love, but we can be willing to fall, with an open, soft, and ready heart. A heart that is hardened cannot be touched. A closed heart cannot receive the blessings that come its way. When our heart isn't open, even if we think we are in love, it is probably something else (infatuation driven by a desire to possess the other person, for instance).

Our heart closes because we have felt burned and we're

afraid of being burned again. We think we have been let down or taken advantage of by others too often, so we put up our guard. We think open hearts are for chumps. It may be a friend or family member who hurt us, or someone at work, or it may be a whole oppressive and exploitative system. One way or another, everybody feels hurt. One of the reasons my grandmother was so inspiring to me was that despite all the hardships she'd had to face under Communist Chinese rule, she kept her heart open and never gave up on humanity.

Sometimes in the process of becoming "educated," we slide into cynicism and lose touch with our caring heart. When I was at Cambridge I was surprised to see how cynicism was often equated with intelligence and sophistication. If you weren't cynical, you were naive. But we shouldn't confuse cynicism with skepticism. The skeptic is open to being persuaded; the cynic, on the other hand, is uninterested and dismissive—closed, because it's safer that way; closed, because the cynic is afraid people will see how much he doesn't know. There is a danger that in wearing the badge of a cynic we might forget how to take it off, and get stuck with it. Cynicism breeds distrust and distrust breeds loneliness, even bitterness, both known sources of misery. Learning—*daring*—to care is the way to get unstuck from cynicism.

As we saw in Chapter 3, it takes courage to open up and step out of our shell, because then we are vulnerable to being disappointed, judged, and hurt. And it's true—many of the people who are most open are the ones who get the most hurt. Worst of all, sometimes the person who hurt us doesn't even care that we feel hurt. Meanwhile, we feel hurt *because* we care about this person. (When a stranger does us wrong, it doesn't hurt as much.) But, as we saw also in Chapter 3, self-protection can become a habit, alienating us from others and from ourselves. The perils of opening up can seem daunting, but the alternative is not really living. It's not that we won't get hurt again; it's that we can learn to care, feel hurt (or disappointed, or cynical), and know that we'll be OK anyway, that we'll live to care another day. And we can learn, whatever happens, not to make it worse. This is the open, infinite, unconditional, engaged safety of meta-awareness, versus the profoundly limited safety of shutting down.

When I feel hurt, I first try to understand where the feeling is coming from. Instead of reacting, I slow down (quiet the mind) and step back (meta-awareness). Slowing down helps me not rush into judgment, of myself or the other person. Sometimes, I discover the feelings have roots that have nothing to do with the other person. Emotional pain almost always has an element of disappointment, which has to do with certain expectations not being met. Slowing down to examine these expectations, we can see that, often, left to their own devices, they've diverged rather wildly from reality without our having noticed. So, feeling hurt, though it's painful (by definition), can also be an opportunity for self-discovery—a tough sell to a cynic, but something we can ready ourselves for and open up to through practice, if we care to.

How do we open our heart? In addition to the sitting meditations later in this chapter, we use everyday life for practice. Every opportunity for kindness is an opportunity to open and warm our hearts. Every moment we feel uplifted by the kindness of others is an opportunity too. All we need to do when these blessings come our way is to be aware of them, and stay with the experience, rather than just moving on to the next thing.

We can use art too. I remember when I first saw Richard Attenborough's *Gandhi*, in the southern Indian city of Bangalore. The feeling of being lifted to another plane of existence stayed with me for days, during which my experience of the world acquired a qualitatively different texture, as if all sensory input was coming to me not through the usual sense organs, but directly through my open heart. Literature does this for some people. In a memorable scene from the movie *Dead Poets Society* (one of my all-time favorites), the central character, an inspiring teacher played by Robin Williams, shares his vision in a passionate burst: "We don't read and write poetry because it's cute. We read and write poetry because we are members of the human race ... Poetry, beauty, romance, love, these are what we stay alive for."

Or it could be religious writing, or music, or visual art that we open to most readily, depending on our cultural background and individual taste. When it comes to music, for me, there's nothing like Tibetan monastic chanting or Bollywood music of the 1970s and '80s, especially songs by the two famous male vocalists Mohammed Rafi and Kishore Kumar. These are the two musical traditions I grew up with as a child. A few years ago, however, I came across a piece called "Spiegel im Spiegel" ("mirror in mirror"), by the Estonian composer Arvo Pärt. It was recently used as a soundtrack for the trailer of the 2013 Hollywood blockbuster *Gravity*, about two astronauts lost in space. A few simple notes repeat continuously with small variations as if the image in one mirror is being reflected in another mirror, and so on, invoking a sense of infinity. I had never heard anything like it, but this music takes me to a place of tenderness and gives me a feeling of being at home in the world.

Of course, it's possible to use books and movies to retreat from the world. Our intention and dedication practice (Chapter 4) helps us notice whether we're taking in art in ways that serve our true purpose.

A woman in her thirties who did the Stanford compassion training course gave an example of how she had gained courage to venture outside herself, and how good it feels out there:

> "I have always been a really shy person. I think CCT has helped me come out of my shell. I was at a music festival with friends listening to a band when I noticed another band playing nearby with no one in front of their stage. I felt for them. They looked lonely. Before I knew it I had run over to them and started dancing! I started dancing! I have never done that before. One by one people started to come over and before long they had a crowd. The more I practice the more I seem to reach out to people. I think my shell protected me from people, but now I think sometimes I don't need it."[2]

Opening your heart through loving-kindness and compassion meditation

The formal sitting practice we use in our compassion training to help connect with our caring heart, adapted from traditional Buddhist meditation, consists of meditations on loving-kindness and compassion. In Buddhist psychology, loving-kindness and compassion are two expressions of one heart, variations on the essential human theme of caring for one another. Loving-kindness is the wish for someone to be happy, and compassion is the wish for someone to be free from suffering. They're closely related, but the emphasis is different, with different feeling tones as a result. We can think of them as two sides of the same coin. We can think of compassion as a more specific version of loving-kindness, focused on suffering in particular. They are two of the four immeasurables (Chapter 4), and two ways to approach a person's well-being.

The root of these practices goes all the way back to the Buddha himself, more than 2,500 years ago. The famed "Metta Sutta" (discourse on loving-kindness) includes an instruction in the form of a series of aspirations for the heart. We incline our heart (and mind—in Pali, the language of the early Buddhist texts, it's the same word) this way, so that it tends toward wishing happiness for others. The instruction goes:

Wishing: "In gladness and in safety,
May all beings be at ease.
Whatever living beings there may be;
Whether they are weak or strong, omitting none,
The great or the mighty, medium, short or small,
The seen and the unseen,
Those living near and far away,
Those born and to-be-born,
May all beings be at ease!"[3]

Drawing from this seminal discourse, the Buddhist traditions developed systematic meditation practices for cultivating loving-kindness and compassion for all beings. These traditional Buddhist meditations typically begin with ourselves; that is, our natural aspiration for happiness and our wish to be free from suffering. Then, focusing on a loved one, we wish this person joy, happiness, peace (loving-kindness), and freedom from suffering (compassion). From there, in ever-expanding circles of attention, we wish joy, happiness, and peace for a "neutral" person (someone we don't have strong feelings about one way or the other), then to a "difficult" person (someone who, we might say, pushes our buttons), and finally moving toward the largest circle—wishing joy, happiness, and peace for all beings.

But, as we discussed in Chapter 2, in the West starting with ourselves tends to bring the process to a screeching halt. So, here, we start with a loved one, and an "easy target" at that. This is someone we get a warm tingling feeling just thinking about. Our relationship with this person (or animal) is currently uncomplicated enough that bringing him or her to mind evokes predominant feelings of tenderness, affection, and kindness in us. A new parent might choose his infant child. A parent of a six-year-old and a fourteen-year-old who loves both her children equally might reasonably start with the six-year-old if the fourteen-year-old happens to be going through a surly phase. You could choose a beloved grandparent, a close friend, or a cherished pet.

EXERCISE: Loving-Kindness Meditation

In our compassion cultivation training, we do this practice in the form of a guided meditation. You may want to record yourself reading these instructions, if you prefer to keep your eyes closed as you follow:

Choose a comfortable sitting position that lets you relax but keeps you alert. To prepare, take three to five deep breaths, bringing each one all the way down to your abdomen and then gently releasing it.

Follow this with a one- to two-minute breath-counting or simple breath-awareness meditation.

Now think of someone for whom you feel a great amount of uncomplicated affection. If it helps, you can use a photograph of this person (or animal) to bring him or her to mind, but it's not necessary to have a visual image; simply think or feel the presence of this person, as tangibly as possible. If you are able to visualize, try to imagine as vividly as possible this person whom you hold dear and care for deeply. Notice how you feel in your heart as you think of this person. (Here *heart* refers more to the area around your heart than to the physical organ.)

If feelings of tenderness, warmth, and affection arise, stay with them. If no specific feelings arise, don't worry. Just stay with the thought of your loved one. Silently repeat the following phrases, pausing after every line.

May you be happy ...
May you be free from suffering ...

May you be healthy ...
May you find peace and joy.

May you be happy ...
May you be free from suffering ...
May you be healthy ...
May you find peace and joy.

Now refresh the thought of your loved one, engendering feelings of warmth, tenderness, and affection, if you can, and again silently say these phrases. You can repeat the steps of this practice for a little while, say, for three to five minutes.

Next, imagine as you breathe out that a warm light emerges from the center of your heart that carries all your feeling of love and connection. This light touches your loved one, bringing him or her peace and happiness. And once again, silently repeat the phrases.

Now, wishing with all your heart that your loved one achieves happiness, rejoice in the thought of his or her happiness. And stay in this state of rejoicing for a minute.

* * *

You can do the same meditation with a shift from wishing someone happiness to the complementary perspective of wishing freedom from suffering instead. This is the heart of compassion meditation.

Ultimately, you wish all beings freedom from suffering, but the "easy target" for compassion, to help you tap into this special heart quality, will be someone (or some being) you know to be suffering and, as with loving-kindness, with whom you have a fairly uncomplicated (i.e., *schadenfreude*-free) relationship. It's not necessary to know him or her personally—you could take the image of a suffering child you saw in the news, for example, or a homeless person you pass on your way to work. You could think about a family struggling to survive every day with fear in the midst of constant violence. Unfortunately, there's no shortage of tragic examples. Or you could contemplate the suffering of a friend or family member going through a hard time. Again, when you put your mind to it you probably won't lack for candidates. It's the first ("noble") truth of Buddhism that there is suffering in life and that it is real. Do you know someone who is suffering with sickness, painful injury, anxiety, depression, or other mental health problems, relationship struggles, unemployment, substance abuse, loneliness, grief ...? It could be the same person as in your loving-kindness meditation. The key is to make your object as concrete as possible, and put your attention on the suffering.

EXERCISE: Compassion Meditation

Once you have done the preliminary deep breathing, as before, followed by a few breath-counting or simple breath-awareness exercises, proceed like this:

Think of a time when the person you have in mind was going through a difficult experience. Perhaps this person is in the middle of one now. Try to imagine what it feels like. Notice what feelings arise in you as you think of this person suffering. You may feel an aching sensation in your heart, or a sense of unease in your gut, or the urge to reach out and help. If no specific feelings or sensations arise in you, stay with the thought. Whatever feelings or thoughts arise, just observe and stay with them.

Then, imagining the suffering of this person, silently offer the following phrases:

> *May you be free from suffering ...*
> *May you be free from fear and anxiety ...*
> *May you find safety and peace.*

Repeat this practice for a little while, continuing to attend to your breath and keeping this person in mind. Every now and then, refresh the thought of the person, and contemplate his or her suffering and needs. Then silently offer the phrases, as before. In this way, repeat the practice for a while, say three to five minutes.

Then, when you wish to end your meditation, imagine as you breathe out that a warm light emerges from the center of your heart and touches the person you have in mind. As it does so, imagine that this eases the person's suffering, bringing peace and tranquility. Then, with a heartfelt wish that the person be free of this suffering, once again silently repeat the phrases.

> *May you be free from suffering ...*
> *May you be free from fear and anxiety ...*
> *May you find safety and peace.*

* * *

A quiet practice with powerful results

The loving-kindness meditation we see today, especially in the West, was originally adapted from the Theravada Buddhist tradition of *metta* practice. The word *metta* is the Pali equivalent of the Sanskrit word *maitri*, a term that shares etymological connection with the word *mitra*, which means "friend" or "friendliness." One of the people responsible for popularizing a secular loving-kindness meditation in the West is the meditation teacher Sharon Salzberg. In addition to teaching the practice extensively, Salzberg collaborated with researchers, especially the American psychologist Barbara Fredrickson, who was interested in exploring possible clinical applications of loving-kindness meditation.

Fredrickson and her team conducted one of the earliest studies on loving-kindness meditation, with employees from a large software and information technology services company in Detroit. Just over two hundred employees volunteered for the study, half being randomly assigned to the meditation group, and the other half to a wait-list control group. The meditation course consisted of six one-hour sessions on loving-kindness meditation led by an expert, based on instructions from Salzberg.[4]

The authors of the study report, "The findings are clear-cut: The practice of [loving-kindness meditation] led to shifts in people's daily experiences of a wide range of positive emotions, including love, joy, gratitude, contentment, hope, pride, interest, amusement, and awe."[5] The authors argue that positive emotions, which are directly enhanced by loving-kindness meditation, can emerge as "the mechanism through which people build the resources that make their lives more fulfilling and help keep their depressive symptoms at bay." The study also found a significant correlation between positive emotions and other personal benefits such as self-acceptance, positive relations with others, life satisfaction, and purpose in life. The authors conclude, "Simply put, by elevating daily experiences of positive emotions, the practice of [loving-kindness meditation] led to long-term gains that made genuine differences in people's lives."[6]

In a later study, this time recruiting sixty-five faculty and staff members from Fredrickson's own University of North Carolina at Chapel Hill, her team examined the connection between loving-kindness meditation and stress. Participants were randomly assigned to two groups: one wait-listed and the other taking six weekly classes on loving-kindness meditation, led by an expert instructor.

One of the important measures for this study was the participants' heart-rate variability; that is, how toned or responsive an individual's vagus nerve might be. The vagus nerve regulates our heart rate fluctuations in connection with our breathing. Fredrickson chose to focus on the vagus nerve in part because it seems to be relevant to how we connect with one another. Anatomically, this nerve is linked to nerves that are crucial for social interaction, such as making eye contact, tuning our ears to other's speech, and regulating emotional expressions. Past studies have shown how higher vagal tone is associated with feelings of closeness to others and with altruistic behavior. (Greater vagal tone as indexed by higher variability of heart-rate is also associated with a lower risk of heart disease, and the vagus nerve plays a role in regulating glucose levels and in our natural immune responses. If it helps us understand connections between all these things—social interaction, altruism, a healthy heart, and our immune system—no wonder people are studying the vagus nerve.)

Compared to those in the wait-listed group, people in the meditation class showed increases in positive emotions and a sense of connection with others, and in vagal function.[7] Reflecting on the results of her study, Fredrickson observed, "Every interaction we have with people is a miniature health tune-up."[8]

The effects of the compassion cultivation training course at Stanford have now been measured on a wide range of outcomes, from emotion regulation to stress response, and from social phobia to PTSD. We will look at some of these findings in later sections of this book.

Personally, one of my favorite benefits from loving-kindness and compassion practice is that it helps counter jealousy and resentment. Few of us will admit, even to ourselves, that we are jealous. But in today's competitive culture, jealousy is quietly pervasive. It even creeps into our homes, as when spouses feel jealous of each other's success. Loving-kindness and compassion practice, since it is basically wishing other people well, conditions us to take joy in their good fortune. This is the most powerful antidote to the problem of jealousy and resentment.

Left unaddressed, jealousy can turn into resentment, and resentment closes our heart. So it's important to not let our feelings of resentment go unchecked. The first step is to recognize it, name it, and then examine where it is coming from. If we need to have a candid conversation with the person triggering our jealousy, we should do so, for the sake of both parties.

The real victim of jealousy, though, is ourselves. The instant jealousy arises, we lose our equilibrium and feel uneasy. Somehow, something isn't quite right. There is a restless energy about it, and we wish it would go away. But trying to deny our feelings of jealousy is like trying not to think about an elephant sitting in the room—we can't help but think about it. Dwelling on it, we may become bitter, and spread bitterness like toxic fumes. We might speak badly about the other person. We might even take pleasure in that person's misfortune. This is the opposite of loving-kindness and compassion, and loving-kindness and compassion are the cure. A beloved verse from my own Tibetan tradition, from a well-known text by the first Panchen Lama, has the following lines:

> *As for suffering I do not wish even the slightest;*
> *As for happiness I am never satisfied.*
> *In this there is no difference between others and me.*
> *Bless me so that I may take joy in other's happiness.*[9]

There is more to loving-kindness and compassion than wishing

In traditional Tibetan practice, loving-kindness and compassion meditation include, in addition to wishing others happiness and freedom from suffering, a deep reflection on the kindness of others. In essence this is a form of gratitude practice, to cultivate a sense of gratitude to those who have been kind to us, especially our loved ones. Today, thanks to a growing body of scientific studies, people in the West are more aware of the positive benefits of gratitude. Cultivating gratitude has been linked to greater well-being as well as increased prosocial behavior.[10] What I like about gratitude is how it puts us in a more positive frame of mind. When our perspectives are tempered by gratitude, we appreciate our good fortune; we treasure what we have rather than bemoan what we don't have, and this tends to make us more optimistic about the future too.

Given the traditional Asian value of honoring the elders, and our parents in particular, the Tibetan practice of reflection on others' kindness takes our mother as a central focus. If we can develop a profound sense of gratitude toward our mother for her kindness, we can extend this to others by recognizing that, through rebirth, countless others have been at various points our mother. To offer a taste of this traditional reflection on the kindness of others, let me quote instructions from a well-known fourteenth-century Tibetan text:

> Whether I was in her womb, being born, or growing up, she fed me and clothed me. She gave me her most precious belongings. She acted as though the status of a universal monarch would be inadequate for me ... To the best of her ability she protected me from dangers and led me to happiness. She is therefore a source of great kindness. So, on my part, too, to reciprocate her kindness, I must protect her from suffering and lead her to happiness.[11]

I once heard the American Buddhist scholar Robert Thurman say that whenever he got really worked up from seeing

President George W. Bush on TV (a "difficult" person for him—this was during the peak of the Iraq crisis following the U. S. invasion), he would try to see his mother's face on the president. He said that it really helped him calm down.

So far, no secularized version of this Tibetan practice exists. But we can take the general point of assuming kindness in others, and paying attention to it when it happens. We can practice making lists of kind things people have done for us, rather than lists of complaints.

There is, however, a formalized Japanese practice known as Naikan, which is taught in the secular setting and is quite similar in spirit. The name Naikan literally means "inside looking"; the technique is a highly structured form of self-reflection designed by a businessman by the name of Yoshimoto Ishin in postwar Japan. Proponents of this practice believe that Naikan helps us understand ourselves as individuals as well as our important relationships in our lives.

On the surface Naikan is a simple practice structured—one might even say quite rigidly—around three questions:

- "What have I received from this person?"

- "What have I given to this person?"

- "What trouble and difficulties have I caused to this person?"

In the traditional format, because of its Asian roots, the practitioner focuses on his or her mother. But in another cultural setting, such as in the West, the focus could be anyone.

Although I have never done the practice, I have had the good fortune of knowing one of the principal researchers of this technique, the Japanese-American anthropologist Chikako Ozawa-de Silva, of Emory University. Chikako understands Naikan to be primarily a form of "mindfulness of others' kindness."[12] In addition to being a researcher, she has done several retreats and attests to the technique's powerful effect. In retreat settings, she told me, people break down in tears with feelings of deep remorse, yet come out at the end with a sense of freedom and deeper commitment to the important relationships in their lives.

It comes back to connection again

The pain of separation, the disappointment of not getting what we want, dissatisfaction with where we are, and the constant hope for something better are among the fundamental conditions that define each one of us as humans. But this vulnerability is also our gift: It equips us to understand others; it makes it possible for us to get out of ourselves and into someone else's skin, as it were. The more we learn to be with our suffering, the more we will be able to connect with other people. ("In this there is no difference between others and me.") Conversely, when we relate to our own suffering with unawareness or resistance, we lose that common ground that lets us connect with others and care for them. So we suffer more.

At a teacher-training retreat for our Stanford compassion course, one of the participants asked, "Since our experience of suffering is so central to our capacity for compassion, isn't there a contradiction in wishing that others be free from suffering?" This is a profound question. I answered that in wishing others freedom from suffering, we're connecting with their natural aspiration for happiness and wanting to be free of suffering. In reality, as human beings we may never be totally free from suffering, and in this sense, it's an academic question. One might say we'll deal with the "problem" of freedom from suffering if and when it happens! In any case, compassion is about how we all *relate* to suffering, our own and others'— suffering we've experienced, are experiencing, or might experience in the future—as much as it is about the fact of suffering. We could be "free" from actual suffering and still be afraid of when it might happen again (in which case we're not really free from suffering, so compassion would still be quite relevant)—this is the extra dimension of suffering that we often bring to our experience, which we could do without. This is what we care about.

The eighth-century Buddhist author Shantideva identifies an important benefit of suffering.[13] He states that our experience of suffering teaches us humility and makes us more empathetic toward others who are suffering. The Nobel Peace laureate and the architect of South Africa's amazing Truth and Reconciliation initiative, Archbishop Desmond Tutu, beautifully captures this insight when he writes, "It is through weakness and vulnerability that most of us learn empathy and compassion and discover our soul."[14] Although we might never be free of pain and suffering, how we respond to suffering can have a huge impact, both for ourselves and for those around us. In the face of suffering, we can give up and wallow in (self-)pity and despair. Or we can close up and harden our heart. Alternatively, we could choose to be with our predicament and emerge from our experience a little wiser, a little more patient, and a little kinder. Compassion practice helps us choose this wiser course, in our engagement with the very human condition of suffering.

7

"May I Be Happy"
Caring for Ourselves

If I do not have peace myself, how can I help others find it?

—Tsongkhapa (1357–1419)

We say of some things that they can't be forgiven,
or that we will never forgive ourselves.
But we do—we do it all the time.

—Alice Munro

Often, we are our own difficult person. If Chapter 2—about how hard it is to be kind toward ourselves in our competitive, individualistic culture and fragmented society—was the bad news, then this is the good news, what we can do to learn self-compassion and self-kindness, even if they don't come easily at first. In this chapter, we tap into the same source we found in the previous chapter—our very own open heart—this time for ourselves. We use, for reference, the loving-kindness and compassion we readily have for "easier" people (*this* is what it feels like), and try to re-create them with ourselves in mind. Our hearts have practiced opening, and now we learn to open them to ourselves.

Self-compassion and attachment style

We all have the capacity for self-compassion, but we don't all relate to it the same way. According to researchers in the field, our differences have a lot to do with the self-protection mechanisms we acquire to deal with challenges and disappointments in our life. Child development and personality studies say the activation and development of what scientists call the *affiliative system* in the first few years of a child's life is critical. The affiliative system, or caring system, as it is sometimes called, is associated with feelings of safety, connectedness, and contentment and is linked to our natural production of opiates and hormones such as oxytocin (sometimes referred to as "the cuddle hormone"). Through a parent's nurturing care, ideally, a baby comes to recognize its parents as sources of reassurance, soothing, and safety. From these early experiences, the baby forms emotional memories of safety, soothing, and calming. The baby feels secure and doesn't forget it. In this happy scenario, the baby would be blessed with what psychologists call a secure attachment style. Drawing on the work of John Bowlby and Mary Ainsworth, contemporary attachment theorists speak of four main styles: secure, anxious and preoccupied, dismissive and avoidant, and fearful and avoidant.[1] But attachment styles aren't just for babies; the concept applies to those early years *and* how they affect our personality, specifically how we relate to the people we're attached to throughout our lives.

As we grow up, some researchers say, our capacity to soothe ourselves develops from those early experiences—a process of emotional remembering, if you will.[2] Deep down, if we have a secure attachment style, we believe that we are safe and OK, or at least we believe in the possibility, because we have known it before. Ideally, those memories stay with us like a mental security blanket in times of stress. So, our attachment style affects our emotion-regulation habits, which affect our baseline self-compassion into adulthood.

If our early experiences were less than ideal, as adults we have to generate that warmth and security from scratch. It's not easy, but it's very possible, because we already have the raw material—our experience of suffering and our natural human capacity for compassion. We can't change our parents or our experiences as babies raised in a particular culture, but as adults we can learn different ways of regulating our emotions and practices to develop our self-compassion. If we are not one of the lucky "secure" ones, we can learn to have compassion for ourselves for this! At the same time, our personality may be more flexible and amenable to change than we think.

Learning to be with our suffering

In compassion cultivation training, we divide the self-compassion practice into two parts. In the first, *cultivating compassion for ourselves*, we learn how to relate compassionately to our own suffering and needs. The second, *cultivating loving-*

kindness toward ourselves, deals with how we relate to our happiness and aspirations. (You'll recognize these two parts from the previous chapter.) The goals are to cultivate, respectively, our capacity to genuinely accept and care for ourselves, and a profound appreciation of our natural and legitimate aspiration to happiness.

In our classes on self-compassion, we ask questions such as: "What would it feel like if we related to our own suffering with more openness and acceptance instead of denial and self-pity?" "What might it feel like to be tender and caring toward ourselves instead of judgmental and self-recriminating?" Class participants discuss how they might reframe their responses to difficulty and suffering in their lives in more compassionate ways. The specific answers aren't as important as the awareness they develop in the process of answering—awareness of their habitual harsh, judgmental reactions; seeing that there might be other, more compassionate ways of relating to their experience; and, in the safety of the class, testing how this feels.

Often, when we are having a hard time we try to ignore the feelings that go with it. This is perfectly natural and understandable. We want to avoid pain. We're afraid that we might fall apart if we do not "pull ourselves together"; that is, suppress our feelings at all costs. This approach is, however, neither healthy nor sustainable in the long run. It costs too much. In many ways, our emotional wounds are similar to our physical wounds. If we suppress emotional pain it will fester like an untreated wound and develop into something worse than the original injury—bitterness, for example, or irritability with and disconnection from others, including those we care about most.

One class participant put it like this:

"I have had some quiet struggles with my feelings lately. Feelings of anger, frustration, disgust, indignance, irritability—all work-related. These feelings did not want to go away or maybe I did not want them to go away. My ego got hurt. I was ready to explode or implode, not sure which one would have relieved me. I was ashamed and angry with myself for having so little control of my feelings and for the thoughts that I had. I rejected compassion. I was done being nice to people (that came out of anger). I felt out of balance with the Universe. I was so mad that needless to say I could not get myself to meditate. So I decided to go to class to see if the turmoil in me could calm down. It did not start very well. I did not want to go to sad places."[3]

Who among us can't relate to these words? Could any single thing that happens at work possibly be as bad as the way we torture ourselves over it for days, weeks, or even years? The participant went on to describe how his heart had opened during a meditation in class, and the anger had "melted away." Reflecting on this, he said:

"The best part is that I still have the same problems at work, same unpleasant situation, and same irritable coworker, but there are no feelings attached. I have been thinking about the same things that trigger my anger and frustrations and ... I can't get angry."

As sentient creatures, suffering is an inescapable part of our reality, and the sooner we can develop a healthy relationship to it the better off we will be. The first step is to learn how to be with our own pain and suffering, without resistance and without giving in to the urge to find an immediate solution. To undo our old emotional habits, we need to do several things: One is to learn the skill of simply observing our experiences and staying with them as they unfold—we need meta-awareness (from Chapter 5) of our suffering.

Another technique, especially for those who may be less inclined toward silent sitting meditation, is learning to distinguish between the language of "observation" and that of "evaluation" or judgment in our thoughts.[4] Observation statements relate to facts, while evaluative statements pertain to our interpretations of these facts. Take the example of going through an airport security check. The line you happened to choose suddenly becomes slower, and you start to get impatient. Because of this you might start thinking, "I always choose the wrong line!" "Why are the security guards being so slow suddenly since I got in the line?" "The guards don't give a damn if people miss their flights." "Nothing ever goes right for me." If we examine them carefully, none of these statements is actually about the facts. They are emotionally charged prejudices, assumptions, and generalizations—our reaction to what is actually happening, which is simply this: There is a slowing down in the checking process. That's all.

We need to challenge our evaluative thinking and other habitual thought patterns, especially our self-concept ("Nothing ever goes right for me"). Despite all the evidence to the contrary from psychology, neuroscience, and our personal experience, most of us continue to hold on to a static self-representation. Each of us has internalized, from our cultural, social, and childhood experience, a particular representation of ourselves, a self-concept that exerts a powerful influence on our everyday life, because it affects how we perceive as well as experience ourselves and the world around us. There's nothing wrong with having a self-concept; the problem is that most of us fail to appreciate that it is just that—a *concept*, a construct of our mind developed through our experience. We believe in the story that we ourselves have made up, and confuse the content of our thoughts with reality. When we catch ourselves indulging in habitual negative self-judgments—"I am no good," "Nobody loves me," "I don't deserve to be happy," and so on—right there, we need to bring in the questioning voice that says, "Wait a minute! These are just my thoughts, not me."

In a remarkable book, David Kelley, the founder of IDEO and the Hasso Plattner Institute of Design at Stanford, speaks of how our own rigid self-concept (in this case, "I am not creative") is often the main obstacle preventing us from expressing our natural creativity.[5] David and his coauthor and brother, Tom Kelley, recount inspiring stories of how when people are able to let go of this fixed mind-set within an environment that encourages fearless expression, their artistic and creative side comes out quite effortlessly. A key lies in what David evocatively calls *creative confidence*, a self-concept that claims creativity as a natural-born human ability in all of us. In compassion too, there is a kind of fearless confidence we can take from knowing that the capacity for it is already in us. This can help break through the doubts and fears that often block us from expressing the kinder part of ourselves.

Cultivating self-forgiveness

To be truly kind and compassionate toward ourselves, we need to examine how accepting and forgiving we are of ourselves. When we have feelings of resentment or enmity toward someone, we cannot generate genuine compassion and concern for that person. The same is true of ourselves. And just as understanding leads to forgiveness for others, understanding our thoughts and actions in terms of the human condition can also give rise to self-forgiveness. We're only human. We're doing the best we can. We need that self-understanding and the self-forgiveness that flows from it. Marshall Rosenberg, the founder of the nonviolent communication (NVC) method, captures this insight: "An important aspect of self-compassion is to be able to empathetically hold both parts of ourselves, the self that regrets a past action and the self that took the action in the first place."[6]

When we judge ourselves harshly and refuse to forgive ourselves for something we have done, essentially, we are attacking the part of us that did that thing—"part" of us in the sense that there were reasons why we did that thing that, consciously or unconsciously, meant something to us. Our evaluative, self-hating mind would say "bad" reasons, but really they were just human reasons. Or perhaps our strategy is to try to amputate this part of us, and those reasons, by denying they exist. (We "just won't think about it." Or, "I'm not the kind of person who does that kind of thing.") Either way, we are at war with a part of ourselves, disconnected from it, and there's no hope of understanding and reconciliation so long as we are at war. Without understanding our (whole) selves, we can't accept our (whole) selves, and without understanding and acceptance we can't learn from our mistake. It may help to think of it in terms of someone else: In the midst of fighting with someone or refusing to acknowledge him, it's safe to say we're not learning from him. Of course, when we don't learn from our mistakes we tend to repeat them, and the battle with ourselves goes on.

Note that, as when we speak to other people, tone matters a lot when we speak to ourselves. We can scream, "How could you do this?!" with the implication "You *monster*!" Or we can gently ask ourselves, "Hmm, let's see, how *did* you do this?" The implication: "What a mess. Let's see how this happened, so hopefully it won't happen again, and I'll help you clean it up."

In CCT, we use specific exercises aimed at self-acceptance and self-forgiveness. They help us explore the possible needs or reasons underlying something we've done, and use this understanding to defuse our self-reproachful reaction. Once we connect to our underlying need, we may have any number of feelings—sadness, frustration, regret, disappointment, hopelessness, and so on. These feelings, which are inherently more accepting feelings—it's sad, *and* it happened—help us move away from guilt, self-recrimination, and negative judgment, feelings that preclude self-acceptance. ("How could I allow such a thing to happen?" "I can't stand myself for letting this happen," et cetera.) Through understanding and acceptance we empathize with ourselves, not only for the thing we did

("Oh yeah, I see how I could have done that"), but for the painful way we reacted to it. (A hazard of learning these skills is that we can turn them against ourselves, and judge ourselves harshly for not being better at these skills!) In NVC language, this process of connecting with the unmet needs is referred to as *mourning*. Mourning gives us permission to regret, which Rosenberg says "helps us learn from what we have done without blaming or hating ourselves."[7]

EXERCISE: Forgiving Ourselves

In our compassion training, we lead the participants through a guided meditation to help engender genuine self-forgiveness:

To do this guided meditation, readjust your sitting position so that you feel comfortable and relaxed. Take three to five deep breaths, bringing each one all the way down to your abdomen and then gently releasing it. Pause for about twenty to thirty seconds in silence.

Now think of a time when you did something that you wish you hadn't, and as a result, you reproached yourself for it. Perhaps you snapped at someone you love and later felt bad about it. Or it could be something that affected only you, such as overspending on something you bought and feeling guilty and ashamed after. Recalling the specifics of the incident is not important, unless they help you to evoke the emotional reaction you felt then. What is important is the recollection of how you engaged in negative self-judgment. Silently stay with this reflection.

Then ask yourself, "Why is it that I reacted so harshly then?"

"What was the unmet need I was trying to fulfill when I did this thing?" When you lost your temper, it could be that you needed respect and felt disrespected by the other person. Perhaps you needed to be heard and felt that this was not happening. Stay with these reflections for a little while.

Now, recognize that although what you did (for example, using abusive language) was not skillful, the underlying need that prompted your action was legitimate. In the case of overspending and feeling ashamed about it, although what you did was unskillful, there again was an underlying need—perhaps you were feeling disempowered and down, and needed a psychological boost. With awareness, allow yourself to experience feelings such as sadness, disappointment, and remorse rather than guilt and shame. Pause with these feelings.

As you touch upon the underlying need that led to the action that brought about the negative self-judgment, stay with it for a while.

Now, breathing out slowly and completely, let go of any tension in the body, let go of any tightness in the mind, and, reflecting on your earlier self-reproachful thoughts, silently say to yourself, "I can let this go. I will let it go."

Finally, imagine that you feel free and expansive in your chest, and then breathe out fully a few more times.

* * *

Self-acceptance

Unfortunately, for most people in our modern culture the feeling of being totally accepted as we are, "warts and all," is rare, if not completely elusive. If we are lucky we might have someone in our life with whom we feel or have felt completely at ease. It could be a grandparent, a favorite teacher from our school years, a spiritual mentor, or one or (if we're really lucky!) both parents, someone who gives us unconditional acceptance. Such a person makes us feel that his regard and affection for us are not contingent upon what we have achieved in life or something we need to do for him; rather, we feel that they go straight to our very being.

A spiritual tradition can also give you a sense of unconditional acceptance. In my own case, I find the visualization of the Buddha of compassion, with his thousand arms and thousand eyes to tend to countless beings, a powerful source of comfort. The only criterion I need to satisfy to be worthy of his care, concern, and compassion is that I am a sentient creature, nothing more. In fact, in Buddhism one epithet for the Buddha means "a loving friend even to a stranger," because his compassion is not contingent on any prior history of personal relationship. The simple fact of being is enough.

Acknowledging the power of this attitude, the British psychiatrist Paul Gilbert developed a practice called *developing a compassionate image*, adapted from Tibetan meditation on the Buddha of compassion.[8] Gilbert, who works with individuals with high shame and excessive self-criticism, attributes these problems to the formation of a self-protective threat response system that is unconstructive, or "maladaptive," in scientific language. According to Gilbert, these people have somehow acquired an emotion regulation style that doesn't use the brain's caring system. The goal in his therapy is to teach them how to activate their caring system and direct it toward themselves.

In CCT too, we use a form of compassion image practice. The core of this technique is to cultivate an image to which we can attribute qualities such as love, compassion, wisdom, steadfastness, trustworthiness, and so on. It needs to be an image with which you feel deep personal connection. It could be that of a wise person whom you admire and respect; it could even be the image of a pet who loves or loved you unconditionally, who, for you, embodied these qualities; it could be the image of a light at your heart, or the image of an expansive and deep blue ocean; it could be a firmly rooted tree with magnificent thick foliage; or if you are a religious person, it could be an icon that is meaningful for you. Whatever image we choose, we practice evoking it in formal sitting practice. The more readily we can call it up, the stronger our sense that it is there for us, not just in sitting meditation, but in everyday life.

EXERCISE: Accepting Ourselves

Once again, take three to five deep breaths, bringing each one all the way down to your belly and then gently releasing it. Pause for a little while—twenty to thirty seconds—in silence.

Now bring to mind an image of compassion that represents for you love, caring, wisdom, and strength. Take a little while to let this thought of your compassion image permeate your mind. It's not necessary to have an actual visual image of a person in the photorealistic sense; but to have the felt sense of the person's presence.

Now imagine that in the presence of this image you feel completely yourself—nothing more, nothing less. There is no need for pretense; there is no need for you to try to be someone other than yourself. There is no judgment, no critical voice; instead, what you find is simply acceptance, warm and tender. Dwell on this feeling of receiving unconditional acceptance. What does it feel like? Do you feel the slowing of your heart, a release of tension somewhere in your body, a sense of letting go?

Retain this compassion image as you breathe. Then, as you breathe in, visualize warm light rays emerging from your compassion image that touch all parts of your body. As these light rays touch you, imagine that they soothe you, ease your suffering, and give you strength and wisdom. Remain with this thought for a while in silence.

Repeat this sequence of imagining light rays emitting from the image and touching you, inspiring feelings of safety, serenity, and total ease in you.

* * *

If you find that this image practice doesn't resonate with you, you could try an alternative method that John Makransky, a Buddhist studies colleague, calls *benefactor moments* in a program he developed called "innate compassion training." Benefactor moments are instances in our life when we felt seen, heard, and recognized by someone who showed us genuine regard and affection. It could be an expression of concern from someone at a difficult time in our life, a sense of "everything's right with the world" we have felt in the presence of an old friend, or simply a warm hug. It could be time we spent with someone we loved to be near as a child.

What characterizes these moments is that they make us feel that we matter; they lift us up, make us feel honored and alive. "Benefactor here means," writes Makransky, "someone who has sent us the wish of love, the simple wish for us to be well and happy;"[9] he underscores the point that benefactors need not be infallible. In the meditation, we bring to mind the image of our benefactor and imagine her sending us her wish for our deepest well-being, happiness, and joy. Whether we use the compassion image technique or the benefactor moments approach, the key is to evoke the feeling of unconditional acceptance in the presence of someone or something that makes us feel easeful and secure. With practice, we gradually expand our circle of benefactors.

Self-kindness

So many of us feel less patient with ourselves than we would be with someone else, less forgiving of our own mistakes, and less able to view ourselves with positive regard. In self-compassion practice, we learn to change this and extend our natural kindness and concern to ourselves. We open up the circle of compassion we have created (Chapter 6), and let ourselves in.

A visualization practice that helps many people to evoke their natural sense of concern and tenderness for themselves is to imagine themselves as a child and then allow their natural feeling toward this child unfold. We might refer to a photo if it helps us get this perspective on ourselves. In CCT classes we use this meditation:

EXERCISE: Self-Kindness

Imagine yourself as a small child, a toddler, perhaps, free yet vulnerable, running around and often knocking things over along the way. Or, if it is more helpful, imagine an age that you can remember from your childhood. Wouldn't you feel instinctively protective toward this child? Instead of negative judgment, criticism, and reprimand, wouldn't you feel tender and caring?

Let these feelings of tenderness and caring toward your child-self permeate your heart, and then silently repeat the phrases:

> *May you be free from pain and suffering . . .*
> *May you be free from fear and anxiety . . .*
> *May you experience peace and joy . . .*
> *May you be free from pain and suffering . . .*
> *May you be free from fear and anxiety . . .*
> *May you experience peace and joy.*

* * *

A colleague who is a senior instructor of Stanford compassion training, Margaret Cullen, shared with me a moving story from her class.[10] In one of the numerous compassion courses Margaret has taught to cancer support groups in the San Francisco Bay Area there was a man enrolled with his wife, a cancer patient. When the eight-week course began, she was wearing a rather intimidating-looking plastic cast on her whole torso—it seems her cancer had metastasized to her bones. The couple were in their seventies and very affectionate with each other. Toward the end of the course, the wife stopped coming because she was too sick to leave her house. However, the husband continued to participate because he was finding the classes helpful to him in his everyday task of looking after his sick wife.

The group had just finished self-compassion exercises the previous week, which included this guided meditation on one-self as a child. During the class check-in, when participants share their experience from the week, the man said that he went back to find a sense of himself as a child and recovered the sense that he was lovable. He had a picture of himself in his parents' arms and felt happy and open-hearted to himself as a baby. He fast-forwarded several years later to a memory of a Christmas that was happy. The family was in Minnesota, there was snow, and he shared various details about the memory that made him feel good. From then on, he saw the difficult things that had happened in his life had turned him into the man that he is today. He felt the pain and saw how he had shut down as a result, and then he felt compassion for the man. He understood why he was protecting himself. He decided that he didn't need to live that way anymore, defensive and shut down. He thought, "What can be the worst that can happen?" After his insight, this elderly, fairly straitlaced man went into the world having decided he would share his heart with whomever he met. Speaking about his wife's cancer, he said, "I've never had any trouble feeling compassion for others but for myself is another matter." The invitation to picture himself as a young boy allowed this cascade of compassion. He felt a weight on his back lift; he felt energized and free.

Since our objective is to change the very way in which we relate to ourselves—how we perceive ourselves, our attitude toward ourselves, how we relate to our needs and predicaments, and how we feel about ourselves—short sitting practices will not be enough. As with cultivating our intention, attention, and loving-kindness, we need to bring our transformative practices into our day-to-day life. In CCT, we speak of "informal practices," when we use everyday life situations as occasions to apply our transformative practices. We recommend three informal practices for self-compassion:

1. Try to be more aware of any negative, self-critical thoughts and self-talk.
2. See that these are just thoughts, constructs, and interpretations; they are representations and not actual facts.
3. Explore ways in which you can reframe negative judgments with more compassionate ones.

Say you do something that you regret, and you launch into unhelpful self-talk ("You idiot!" "How could you do that again?" "You are a loser.") When this happens, the first step is to notice what is happening—that you have slipped into negative self-judgment. Meta-awareness practice helps with this. Next, can you see that these labels you are throwing at yourself are really just your thoughts, constructed out of frustration and disappointment in yourself? Finally, can you reframe these thoughts in a more constructive way? Instead of beating yourself up with "You loser," "You are an idiot," "How can anyone love you?" you could reframe these as "Slow down," "You are in pain," "You need assurance," and so on. When you speak your truth this way, your heart will know it. Reframing the language of self-judgment as self-kindness, especially if you keep at it on a regular basis, can be a powerful source of personal transformation.

So, through these reflections and exercises, we can learn to be more accepting, forgiving, and caring toward ourselves, and less negative and judgmental of our perceived failings and misfortune—that is, to be more self-compassionate. However, to be truly self-compassionate, we also need to have a healthy relation to our legitimate needs and basic aspirations as humans. We need to have, as it were, a gut-level appreciation of our basic humanity, our need for love and happiness. This, then, is the focus of the second part of the self-compassion practice.

Loving-kindness for ourselves

As we did with compassion from the previous chapter to this one, turning it from others toward ourselves, we will do with loving-kindness too. You'll recall, loving-kindness is the side of caring that manifests as wishing someone happiness. It is warm, caring, tender, and connected, and hopeful of success and joy. Loving-kindness is also unconditional, nonjudgmental, and open. Loving-kindness for ourselves should be a most natural thing, an expression of our fundamental disposition: the wish to be happy and avoid suffering.

One complication is that many people believe that focusing on ourselves is inherently selfish or narcissistic. The truth is, if anything, loving-kindness for ourselves makes us more aware of and empathetic toward other people's feelings and needs.

Nurturing and soothing ourselves is rejuvenating, so that we have altogether more benevolent energy for relating to others and the world around us. When we feel full of heart, we also tend to be more generous in our treatment of others. When we give ourselves the loving-kindness we need, we get the sense that there is plenty to go around, and that we have more to give.

One way to begin is to clarify our deeper aspirations. We can do this through sitting, journaling, discussion, or some combination of these. When there is a quiet moment in our day, we can ask ourselves, as we did in Chapter 4 when we set intentions, "In my heart of hearts, what do I really want in my life?" If we repeat this process over time, we may find that values we cherish can actually become the goals of our aspirations. We recognize that, deep down, we aspire to genuine happiness—for meaning, for wholeness, for inner peace, for fulfillment—and that this aspiration is a fundamental aspect of our being. When we honor our wish for happiness, it becomes a tremendous inner resource. And because this wish comes from the core of our humanity, by embracing it we embrace everyone who shares it, which is to say: everyone.

Another way into loving-kindness for ourselves is to pay attention to the good things in our lives and rejoice in them. It could be something that we did, or something about ourselves that we feel good about. It could be our good fortune of having a loving partner, a family, or a community. It could simply be our zest for life. If nothing specific comes to mind, we can rejoice in the natural capacity for empathy and kindness that we possess as human beings. I heard the Dalai Lama once remark, "I celebrate my life as a human, if for nothing else, for the simple ability it gives me to sing praises of altruism." This practice of counting our blessings is proven to have important health-related benefits. The challenge is to avoid sliding into self-satisfaction, which only inflates our ego, and to stay with genuine rejoicing that is an expression of true gratitude.

Replenishing our inner wellspring

Among the military veterans at the Palo Alto residential treatment center for PTSD, where CCT has been on offer now for two years, there was a Vietnam veteran.[11] He found the self-compassion component of the course so meaningful that in addition to following the in-class self-compassion meditations, he took opportunities throughout the day to engage in these meditations, especially when he participated in other group (including trauma group) activities. Since he suffered from extreme insomnia anyway because of his condition, he started using the late-night hours for self-compassion meditations as well. He said that he realized his decades-long abusive relationship with substances came about because he did not know how to access this feeling of holding himself and his painful war experiences in a compassionate way. The way he spoke about what it feels like to have self-compassion and the vulnerability underlying his substance use, I was truly moved.

A mother in a CCT workshop talked about how, through self-compassion, she saw that she had been out of relationship with herself for a long time.[12] She had been so focused on taking care of everyone else that, in the process, she forgot her own feelings and needs. Paradoxically, she realized, neglecting herself made her less emotionally available to her family. The self-compassion practices helped her to reconnect with herself. Now she wants to find a way to share this insight with her children so that they too may learn self-compassion.

Prioritizing self-compassion is like the airline safety announcement: "If you are traveling with children, make sure that your own mask is on first before helping your children." The strength of character, courage of heart, and depth of wisdom to be there for other people depends on our compassion for ourselves.

8

"Just Like Me"

Expanding Our Circle of Concern

This virtue, one of the noblest with which man is endowed, seems to arise incidentally from our sympathies becoming more tender and more widely diffused, until they extend to all sentient beings.

—Charles Darwin (1809–1882)

As for suffering I do not wish even the slightest;
As for happiness I am never satisfied.
In this, there is no difference between others and me.
Bless me so that I may take joy in others' happiness.

—First Panchen Lama (1570–1662)

In *The Heart of Altruism*, social scientist Kristen Renwick Monroe recounts a series of interviews she conducted with Jewish rescuers in Nazi-occupied Europe, especially Holland and Denmark, during the early 1940s.[1] The story of two rescuers from Holland, whom Monroe refers to simply by their first names, Tony and Bert, shows how this courageous act was not confined to any specific socioeconomic or religious background. As a son of a doctor and educated mother, Tony grew up in affluence in Amsterdam with frequent sojourns at his family's country house. Bert, in contrast, was raised in a large family in a small town and led a typical "country life of Dutch workers depicted in Van Gogh's portraits."[2] Tony's amazing journey into saving Jews began somewhat casually, when he made the simple suggestion to the father of his Jewish friend to come and stay at their family country house. Bert's, on the other hand, began with hiding a Dutch couple involved in sending Jews to Spain. The first Jewish person Bert hid was a friend of his wife, Annie. Bert and his wife owned a pharmacy in a large building, in which they built a secret room to hide the people they were helping to save from the Nazis. Both Tony and Bert continued with their courageous enterprise over a prolonged period of time, with full awareness of the grave risks they were taking for themselves and their families. Bert was in fact betrayed once by a fellow Dutchman, resulting in an extensive search of his house by German soldiers.

After a lengthy analysis of these interviews, Monroe comes to the conclusion that what united all the rescuers was neither their religious beliefs nor strong ethical standards but what she calls their "perceptions of a shared humanity." She understands this as reflecting "a different way of seeing the world and oneself in relation to others," in which all humankind is perceived to be connected through a common humanity—an attitude the Dalai Lama often characterizes as recognition of "the oneness of humanity." The statements of many of these rescuers Monroe records in her book poignantly capture this notion of the oneness of humanity. When asked if there was anything similar about the people they helped, one of the rescuers responds, "No. They were just people." Another rescuer says matter-of-factly, "A human being who is lying on the floor and is bleeding, you go and do something."[3] Our Dutch rescuer Bert makes this point even more sharply when he says, "You help people because you are human and you see that there is a need. There are things in life you have to do, and you do it."[4]

This theme from Monroe's work—that at the heart of altruism lies the perception of a shared humanity—resonates beautifully with an important insight in Buddhist thought: *What facilitates the arising of empathetic concern for another is a sense of connection—in fact, a kind of identification—we feel with the other*. Pain is such a powerful connector. When we see someone bleeding on the ground, we respond instinctively; we do not stop to think how we should feel about the situation. We act.

The implication is radical: If we learn to relate to others from the perspective of our shared humanity, we could extend our empathetic concern to strangers and even those whom we find difficult to relate to. Buddhist-derived compassion meditations use phrases such as "Just like me, others too wish to attain happiness and overcome suffering" constantly, almost in the fashion of a mantra: "just like me," "just like me ... " Plus, as a consequence of relating to others through our common humanity, we are graced with no end of opportunities to get out of our own head, a key both to compassion and to our personal happiness, as we have seen.

A woman who was a teacher trainee for the Stanford compassion course took on the daily CCT meditations with gusto, every day for at least thirty minutes.[5] As part of "embracing common humanity" practice, she was asked to imagine extending compassion to a difficult person as well. She chose her ex-husband and his girlfriend. Every day she would alternate between them, and she found that it was always a challenge for her. But she knew that this was a *practice* and in time it might help. Nine months into her daily meditation practice, she was following a different guided compassion meditation, and was instructed to visualize her loved ones in front of her. To her surprise, her ex-husband and his new girlfriend appeared! She couldn't believe her eyes, or, rather, her mind. They had turned into her "loved ones." That surprise appearance began a shift in her attitude toward them. She understood that "just like me, they too suffer and want to be happy." As she put it, "I'm not saying my relationship with them is always rainbows and daisies. However, I know the meditations have created peace within me that I can extend toward them. This shift has tremendously affected how I interact with them, which most certainly benefits our seven-year-old daughter, who, because of a shared custody arrangement, lives at both homes."

Now, whether our feelings about others actually lead to some tangible benefit is contingent upon many other factors. Sometimes other people simply may not be ready to receive our help. What cannot be denied, however, is the benefit to ourselves. We feel less lonely. And acknowledging other people's role in our own welfare leads us to see them not as a source of antagonism, but rather as a source of benefit and joy.

The power of perceived similarity

Two American psychologists, Piercarlo Valdesolo and David DeSteno, demonstrated through a creative experiment how perceived similarity, even a trivial one, between us and another person influences our concern and compassion for that person. The study paired two people, one a real participant and the other a confederate (someone hired by the research team), in a series of activities. In the first part, the two participants—sitting opposite each other, each with a computer monitor in front—were asked to tap their hands on sensors as they listened to tunes being played over headphones. The participants had been randomly assigned into two groups, one in which the pairs tapped in synchrony, and one in which the tapping didn't match. The participants then witnessed their tapping partner (the confederate) unfairly assigned to complete a host of boring tasks, and were given the opportunity to help.

What the researchers found was that the simple act of synchronized tapping, for as short a time as three minutes, dramatically influenced the way participants felt about their tapping partner.[6] Those who engaged in synchronized tapping reported feeling greater similarity with their partner; they also displayed greater compassion when their partner was unfairly penalized. Amazingly, 31 percent more participants in the synchronized-tapping group helped their partners with the assigned work than in the out-of-sync group, and they spent an average of more than seven times as long helping. DeSteno writes, "There is nothing special about tapping in synchrony; any commonality will do." Often, he points out, we have a choice: Do we see our neighbor as a different ethnicity, or as a fan of the same local restaurant? The latter will increase our compassion.[7] This study reinforced my conviction in the key Buddhist insight that the marrow of compassion is our identification with the object of our concern.

One area in which the close link between our compassionate concern and our sense of identification with another has been known for some time is charitable giving behavior. "Identifiable victim effect" refers to our preference for giving to individual victims as opposed to anonymous victims of misfortune, suggesting that our identification with the victim influences our compassion for his or her plight. This phenomenon appears to be, in fact, part of a larger psychology of compassion. We tend to feel compassion more easily for real people than for an abstract idea of humanity; for a concrete individual than for a group of people; for someone who is identifiable than for someone who remains anonymous; for someone who is actually suffering than for someone who might suffer. This is the reason why we respond so much more dramatically to a photograph of one individual in distress than we do to statistics that cite thousands of people who need our help.

A colleague at Stanford, psychologist Brian Knutson, and his team recently discovered the neural underpinnings of this identifiable victim effect.[8] They conducted an experiment with Stanford undergraduates using different sets of images. One set included (1) a photo of a child with a name, (2) a photo without a name, (3) a silhouette with a name, and (4) a silhouette without a name; the other set used just two images: a photo with a name and a silhouette with a name. Participants were paid fifteen dollars per hour for their time, as well as an endowment of fifteen dollars paid up front so that they actually had the money in their pockets. They were informed that the researchers had established a partnership with a children's refugee orphanage in the Darfur region of Sudan, for which each subject would be asked to donate from their endowment money. In the experiment, the images were followed by one screen with an amount requested, another with a choice of yes or no, ending finally with a neutral screen. As expected, they found that subjects preferred to give more when the victim was more identifiable—that is, when a photograph was shown rather than a silhouette—also, picture trumped name, as they gave more after a photograph with no name than after a silhouette with a name. When it comes to compassion, our feelings closely follow our perceptions.

So, perceived similarity elicits our natural capacity for empathetic concern. Conversely, when we fail—or, worse, deliberately refuse—to recognize similarities between us and others, we create situations that are totally contrary to our empathetic nature. Whether it's a seemingly innocuous attitude of indifference or full-blown dehumanization of the other, our history attests to the consequences of failing to recognize our similarities. From slavery to the Jewish Holocaust, and from the ethnic cleansing in the Balkans to the Rwandan genocide, at the root of all of these horrors is the lack of perception of a shared humanity. Rather, the victims were subjected to stages of progressive dehumanization, beginning with differentiation of "us" and "them," objectification, and generalization of the other through stereotyping, dehumanization, and, in some cases, demonization.

Embracing our common humanity

This is why we have a step in Stanford compassion training called "embracing common humanity," when we explore the fundamental truth that *just like me*, other people want happiness and do not want suffering. And just like me, others have the right to pursue this fundamental aspiration. The aim in the training is not intellectual assent; rather, it is to embrace this truth in such a way that we feel it, as it were, in our guts.

In CCT, cultivating a sense of common humanity is actually the first of three steps involved in extending our compassion to others in expanding circles of concern—from loved ones (Chapter 6) to ourselves (Chapter 7) to, in this chapter, strangers, difficult people, and, finally, to all humanity. In the first step, we cultivate understanding of the *basic sameness of self and others*, through a deep recognition of the common aspiration for happiness and freedom from suffering that we all share. In the second, we cultivate a sense of *appreciation of others* through seeing how intimately our lives and well-being are interconnected. The third step is the actual practice of expanding our circle of compassion. The challenge in this process is to identify with those who are not close to us.

A major focus for practice is our shared aspiration for happiness: Just as we wish for happiness, so do all others. As part of our training, we use meditations and visualizations.

EXERCISE: Embracing Common Humanity

Imagine someone whom you hold dear, someone you find it easy to care about and love. This could be a family member, such as your young child, an aging parent, or a grandparent; or a close friend. For some, it could be a loving pet. Don't just think about the object of your affection in the abstract; see if you can feel his or her presence.

Notice any pleasant feelings that form within you as you picture this dear one. Now imagine being this person, and see how easy it is for you to acknowledge that he or she has the same aspiration for genuine happiness that you do.

Now bring to mind another person—someone you recognize but have not had significant contact with, for whom you have no special sense of closeness. Think of a real person you see quite often, perhaps someone you see at your workplace or in your class, perhaps a bus driver or someone who works at your local café or library.

Noticing the feelings that may arise in you as you picture this person, see how these feelings may be quite different from the ones you felt in relation to your loved one. Usually we do not concern ourselves with the thought of whether or not such a person is happy. Even when we happen to interact with this person, we do not give much thought to what might be his or her situation. We get what we came for and just move on. But now try to imagine being this person. Imagine his life, his hopes and fears, which are every bit as real, multilayered, and diverse as your own.

Recognize the profound similarity between yourself and this

person at the fundamental human level, and reflect, "Just like me, he wishes to achieve happiness and to avoid even the slightest suffering."

Next, bring to mind a person with whom you may have some difficulty, someone who irritates or annoys you, someone who may have done you harm, or someone you think takes satisfaction in your misfortune. Picture this person in front of you.

If, as a result of imagining this person, you happen to experience uncomfortable feelings, simply acknowledge them. You might recall painful interactions with him or her, how you felt then about uncomfortable feelings that arose in you. Don't suppress the feelings, and don't reinforce them by trying too hard to accurately recall those exchanges ("Then she said ... but I said ... ").

Now put yourself in this person's shoes for a moment, recognizing that she is an object of deep concern to someone, she is a parent or a spouse, a child and a dear friend of someone. Acknowledge that this person has the same fundamental aspiration for happiness that you have. Let your mind remain in this awareness for a little while, say twenty to thirty seconds.

Finally, picture all three people together in front of you, and reflect on the fact that they all equally share a basic yearning to be happy and free from suffering. On this level there is no difference at all between these three people; in this fundamental respect, they are all exactly the same. See if you can relate to each of these three people from that perspective, from this basis of the aspiration for happiness that we all share.

This aspiration for happiness and wish to overcome suffering are a common bond that unites us with all other beings. Let your mind abide in this awareness for a while.

With this deep recognition that the wish for happiness and the wish to overcome suffering are common to all, silently repeat this phrase: "Just like me, all others aspire to happiness and wish to overcome suffering."

* * *

This practice opens the way for more constructive modes of relating to others. There is a reason why so many people loved the movie *E.T.* The humanlike features of the alien, his tragic situation of being stranded on earth, his fear of what might happen to him, and his longing to return home (crystalized in the famous phrase "E.T. phone home"), all set within the context of a deepening friendship with a lonely boy, made it a universal story of empathy and compassion. I appreciated this movie so much that when my two daughters were old enough to transition from children's animation to live-action movies, I chose it as their "grown-up" debut.

Sometimes, the "just like me" practice can work in the most unexpected ways. I heard a moving story from my colleague Leah Weiss, who taught CCT numerous times at the military residential treatment center for PTSD in Palo Alto.[9] One of the participants, an ex-soldier in his mid-forties, said that of all the things he had learned from the compassion training course offered at the center, the contemplation of our common aspiration for happiness was the most immediately helpful. He said that he had struggled with an anger problem for a long time and had undergone all kinds of therapy and treatment, but the course provided him with a valuable tool that supported his healing process. His anger would get triggered particularly when he perceived unfairness on somebody else's part, such as someone queue-jumping in a supermarket or zooming in quickly to snatch a parking space. When this happened, he would go into a rage; he had even assaulted the other person on some occasions. Thanks to compassion training, he said, he now uses the contemplation *Just like me, he too wishes to be happy and avoid suffering*, almost like a mantra to calm himself down. He said that now when he catches himself getting worked up because of something someone has done, he repeats the phrase to himself—"Just like me . . . Just like me . . . "—and it does help him calm down.

A special education teacher and certified CCT instructor described a revelation she'd had about a difficult person at work (emphasis added):

"While I was involved in CCT classes I was dealing with a very challenging and demoralizing situation at work. For the past four years I have been successfully using mindfulness on a daily basis, both personally and with my students in the classroom. However, this daily practice was not sufficient in helping me deal with a very antagonistic and contentious evaluation process with my principal. I truly believe that if I had not been involved with CCT at the time, I very likely would have transferred schools or even left the profession entirely. My weekly classroom observations by this principal resulted in severe and unwarranted criticism of my teaching practices. Our post-evaluation meetings always seemed to occur the day of my CCT classes. For that, I am eternally grateful. Not only did I receive a wealth of support and compassion from my CCT colleagues and trainers; I quickly understood that this principal's behavior was merely a tragic expression of an unmet need. So instead of falling into the victim role, I learned to feel compassion for this woman on a daily basis. She was my "difficult person" *who I knew at the very core was merely trying to be happy and to be loved.* This transformed my overall experience with my principal. I was able to glean the reasonable suggestions she had to improve my teaching practice and ignore all of the vitriolic criticism."[10]

Cultivating appreciation of others

Having embraced our shared humanity in CCT, we then turn to contemplating how deeply interconnected we are. Participants reflect on how our own lives and the lives of countless others are intertwined in a network of relationships that sustain and promote the well-being of everyone who is part of the network. Although contemporary culture tends to promote individualism, independence, and self-reliance, the reality of our life today is such that we are thoroughly social, interdependent, and reliant on others.

Take, for example, the various necessities of our life—the things we require to maintain our life and health and flourish. From the food we eat, the clothes we wear, and the home we live in to the books we enjoy reading, the ideas that inspire us, and the many services we take advantage of every day, we depend on others for every one of our comforts and joys ... and for our very survival. As the Tibetan mind-training teachers remind us, even to enjoy fame we need others to talk about us.[11]

Try tracing the chain of people involved in finally bringing a T-shirt into a local shop, and there will be potentially countless individuals: the farmers who produced the cotton, the workers in the garment industry, the people who helped distribute the products, and finally the salesperson in the shop where we bought the item. There would be the farmers who grew the food that the cotton farmers ate for lunch, and the people who drilled the oil on which the farm machinery runs; people on the ship that brought the T-shirt from where it was made, if it was made overseas, and people to get it off the ship and drive it to the warehouse; couriers who brought the shipment of T-shirts to the shop ... and so on.

Or contemplate the people who may have been involved in making it possible to have a bowl of rice on our table. Having worked in the fields in southern India in my early teens, I always try to appreciate the hardships farmers endure in order to make food available for others, and I teach my daughters to be aware of these too. Plowing, seeding, tending, and harvesting; weather, pests, et cetera—theirs is a tremendously patient work fraught with worries about all sorts of things that can go wrong.

Today, there is the marvelous technique of life cycle analysis, which assesses the environmental impact of a single product, such as the iPhone one has in one's hand.[12] The analysis traces the steps in producing the product, from extraction of raw material to manufacturing of parts, from labor involved in different parts of the world to transportation. This is a powerful tool to help us appreciate the interconnected nature of everyday objects, from smartphones to our favorite jeans, and we can use it to contemplate how dependent we are on others. As we delve into this thoroughly interconnected reality that is our existence, we realize how there is literally nothing that is part of our life—our existence, our welfare, and even our identity as an individual—that does not depend on others.

This interconnectedness of self and others extends to our very identity. Even the most cherished object of our thought, the feeling of "I," is contingent upon the presence of others. "I" can be defined only in relation to "you" and "they"; without others the thought of "I" simply would not arise. In fact, I noticed that it takes quite a long while before a baby learns to use the first-person pronouns like "I," "me," and "mine." As parents we kind of know this intuitively. We say things like, "Will you give it to Daddy?" "Mummy will do this," "Mummy is sad," and so on, using the third person to refer to ourselves. The child does the same. When my daughters were learning to speak, they would refer to themselves in the third person or drop the subject from their sentences ("Want that!"). Developmental scientists speak of how babies' identities are fused with their mothers', and only over time do they acquire an autonomous identity as a separate individual.

In CCT classes, we lead the participants through a guided meditation focused on appreciating others this way.

EXERCISE: Appreciating Others

As you contemplate the various ways in which you are the beneficiary of contributions from so many people, including countless strangers, acknowledge that it's the presence of others that makes it possible for you to live; it's their presence that gives meaning to your existence; and it's their deeds that contribute toward your welfare. Now allow your heart to open so that a sense of appreciation and gratitude may begin to arise in you. Abide in this state, and whatever positive thoughts and feelings you happen to experience, let them permeate your entire being.

Next contemplate this thought: "Just as I feel happy when others wish me well, and feel touched when others show concern for my pain and sorrow, so everyone else feels the same way. Therefore I shall rejoice in others' happiness and feel concerned for their pain and sorrow."

Once again, recalling your profound recognition that others aspire to happiness and shun suffering the same way you do, open your heart to rejoicing in others' happiness and connecting with their pain.

Now—having brought to your mind the fundamental recognition that, just like me, all others aspire to happiness and wish to avoid suffering, as well as having reflected on the deeply interconnected nature of yourself and others—let your heart become permeated by the sense of connection with others.

* * *

Expanding our circle of concern

Here we consciously expand our circle of concern to include not just ourselves and our immediate loved ones, but a much larger group of others as well. In doing so, we break free from what Albert Einstein called the "optical delusion of consciousness"—

our sense of being separate from others and the universe. We learn to transcend our tribal tendency to relate to others in terms of "us" and "them," or in-group and out-group. Einstein, for example, compared our sense of separateness to a prison that restricts us "to our personal desires and to affection for a few persons nearest to us." And our task, he maintained, "must be to free ourselves from this prison by widening our circle of compassion to embrace all living creatures and the whole of nature in its beauty."[13] Here is a meditation to guide us in widening our circle of compassion to embrace all living creatures.

EXERCISE: Expanding Our Circle of Concern

Having settled into a relaxed state, physically and mentally, bring your attention into the present moment by observing your breath. Settle into the only reality there is at this very moment, the present. Let your mind rest simply in the awareness of the gentle rhythm of your breathing.

Now think of a time when you experienced great difficulty and suffered. Notice how you feel when you think of such an experience ... then, with feelings of tenderness, warmth, and caring toward yourself, silently repeat these phrases:

May I be free from suffering ...
May I experience peace and joy.

Next, with a firm recognition that the wish for genuine happiness is an essential part of your being, silently repeat the following phrases:

May I be happy . . .
May I be free from suffering . . .
May I find peace and joy.

With all your heart, stay with these aspirations for a little while, twenty to thirty seconds.

Now picture someone for whom you feel a great amount of affection. Notice the feeling of tenderness and warmth this may bring to your heart and how this makes you feel. Then think of a time when this person was going through difficulty, noticing how you experience a sense of concern based on a feeling of tenderness toward your loved one. Notice how you feel for his or her pain; you may even feel an urge to reach out and help. With these feelings and sentiments, silently recite the phrases:

May you be happy . . .
May you be free from suffering . . .
May you find peace and joy.

Repeating them silently, stay with the sentiments echoed in these phrases.

Now think of someone you neither like nor dislike, someone you might see often but have no particular contact with—someone at your workplace, the gym, or your local café. Reflect how, just like you, he is important in someone's life. Just like you, he seeks love and happiness. Just like you, he has dreams, aspirations, hopes, and fears. Then reflect: "Just like me, he aspires to happiness and wishes to overcome suffering."

Now imagine this person faced with suffering, embroiled in a conflict with a loved one, struggling with an addiction, or suffering deep sadness or depression. Allow your heart to feel tenderness and concern for this person ... if possible, allow your heart to even feel the urge to do something about it. With these sentiments, silently repeat:

May you be free from this suffering ...
May you experience peace and joy ...
May you be free from this suffering ...
May you experience peace and joy.

Now contemplate this thought: "In fact, everyone on this planet, not just myself and those I care about, shares the same fundamental aspiration to happiness and the same wish to overcome suffering. Just like me, everyone wishes to achieve happiness. Just like me, everyone wishes to be free of pain, fear, and sorrow. Just like me, everyone seeks to fulfill their basic aspiration to happiness and freedom from suffering." Stay with this thought for a little while.

Now, filling your heart with the wish that all beings be free of suffering, silently repeat these phrases:

May all beings be free from suffering ...
May all beings be free from pain and sorrow ...
May all beings be free from fear and anxiety ...
May all beings experience peace and joy.

Think of how all these beings, each and every one of them, continue to be afflicted by pain, sorrow, and fear, even though what they aspire to is peace and happiness. Let your heart feel: *How I wish that they were all free from fear and sorrow.*

Infusing your mind with this feeling of compassion, allow it to fill your heart. Be in this state for a little while, listening to the beautiful inner silence.

* * *

This contemplation can be a daily meditation practice. You can record the text in your own voice or have a prerecorded version in someone's voice that you find soothing, and follow the practice by playing it back to yourself. We recommend doing this early in the morning or at a time and place that you know will be comparatively quiet and conducive to a relaxed state of mind. Depending on how you record the script, this daily compassion meditation can be as short as ten to fifteen minutes or as long as thirty to forty-five minutes.

Priming our heart for a more active compassion

One final practice of our compassion training course is what we call *active compassion meditation*. This is an adaptation of the well-known Tibetan practice called *tonglen*, literally "giving and receiving," which involves mentally taking away from others their suffering, misfortunes, and destructive mental states while offering them our own happiness, good fortune, and positive mental qualities. We call this active compassion meditation in CCT because in this practice we are priming ourselves to actually act out our compassionate concern for others. In traditional Tibetan practice, tonglen is often synchronized with breathing. As we breathe in, we imagine taking from others their pain and suffering, including the causes, often visualized as streams of dark clouds or smoke entering our body, where they dissolve into a light. And as we breathe out, we imagine sending out happiness and good fortune.

Tonglen is a practice we can apply both to our own situation as well as to that of others.[14] When we fall ill or suffer misfortune, such as a financial setback, we can apply tonglen meditation. With phrases such as "May this suffering of mine serve to spare others from a similar predicament," we imagine we're taking upon ourselves the same illness or misfortune afflicting many others right at this very moment. The idea is to use the opportunity presented by the universality of suffering to connect with others. The Tibetan flutist Nawang Khechog once suffered a terrible car accident on his way to visit his father in Orissa Tibetan Settlement in eastern India. It was on the eve of the Tibetan New Year and Nawang was traveling with his son and niece. The car they were in was hit by a truck, killing the driver and seriously injuring Nawang's niece, who later died in hospital. Though his son suffered minor injuries, Nawang himself was seriously hurt and had to spend several months in the hospital, undergoing multiple extensive operations. He shared with me that it was his tonglen practice that sustained him in the initial weeks of serious pain and fear of not knowing if he would live. He would spend hours, as he lay in bed, thinking of countless others who are suffering physical injury, emotional trauma, and fear. He would breathe in their suffering, and breathe out his compassion and concern for their well-being. (Nawang recovered completely from the accident and has been able to resume his career as a flutist.)

We can also do tonglen when someone we love is suffering. We can imagine taking away the person's sickness or misfortune and sending her our love and compassion, wishing her to find relief. If, say, you are sitting next to the bed of a loved one who is dying, you can silently imagine taking away her pain and sending waves of light that suffuse her with your affection and kindness, bringing her courage and peace. Doing tonglen in this way allows you to be fully present for your loved one, and retain the focus of your thoughts and emotions on how best to be there for him or her, instead of becoming preoccupied with your own fear about what the death of this person might mean for you. Tonglen is a powerful method to help us connect with—and be courageous in the face of—suffering.

One CCT trainee, a sixty-four-year-old hospital chaplain, told us this story about tonglen:[15]

"It was an ER request for a chaplain because paramedics were bringing in a two-year-old child from a drowning accident. I felt myself cringe inwardly because I knew the magnitude of this kind of situation—the hardest call for all concerned is when it involves a child.

I prayed for strength as I hurried toward the ER. The nurse told me there were two children, siblings, and doctors were performing CPR, but it didn't look good at all. She said the mother was here ... I felt my whole body tighten as I entered the room to see the young mother bent over and sobbing from the depths of her being.

Thus began a series of encounters that personified human suffering: from the health care providers who were unable to revive the children, to the young parents, to the many family members arriving at different intervals to be told the unimaginable news. The whole ER environment was acutely aware of this tragedy, and its effects were tangible; it permeated the atmosphere like a dark cloud.

I felt overwhelmed, as if I was going to collapse under the weight of the suffering and my task. What could I offer? I felt like I could not find a direction for the suffering and was going numb.

Then, I remembered the 'giving and receiving' [tonglen] technique I learned in my CCT class. My first thought was 'Not in the midst of this; there is too much happening right now!'

But I was desperate for a way out. So, I breathed in the suffering as if it were a dark cloud and breathed out golden light from my heart into the room and to everyone I encountered. A whole new level of integration happened. I could open to the experience of suffering and found something necessary and precious to sustain me. The suffering became fluid with each breath and washed over me so that I began to become unstuck. I began to feel the liberation of not being trapped in the experience of suffering, but the freedom that happened as a result of actively engaging in it. This was the gift and I am deeply grateful."

For some people, the idea of consciously taking on others' suffering—even in their imagination—might be too much. The eighth-century Buddhist author Shantideva asked the same question: "Since compassion brings additional pain, why deliberately seek to engender it?"[16] In response, he draws our attention to a psychological difference between the experience of our own suffering and the distress from compassion for someone else's. Unlike our own suffering, the pain occasioned by our compassion for someone else is voluntary. We have a choice, and we choose not to disconnect from the other person's pain. Shantideva compares this to situations like illness, in which for the sake of preventing a more serious problem, we are willing to endure hardships. We go to the dentist. We elect to have surgery. Furthermore, compassionate concern for someone else's situation is a fundamentally empowered state of mind, which prompts us to reach out to the other person. Also—it's worth repeating—by feeling someone else's pain, we get out of ourselves. This in itself is a relief from our own pain and sorrow.

This said, even the Tibetan tradition recognizes that doing tonglen all out right from the start could prove challenging. So we could proceed in a gradual way. We could begin by doing tonglen for our own future self, taking away the pain, fear, and sorrow and sending our loving-kindness, compassion, and whatever strength we might feel right now. For example, we could imagine doing this practice with respect to our self of tomorrow, next month, next year, next decade, and so on. Once we feel comfortable with this practice, we then shift our focus and do tonglen for someone we care about. And as we feel comfortable with this, we gradually expand our focus and include our larger circle of family and friends, and so on.

Overleaf is an example of a guided tonglen meditation for someone else, but, again, you can adapt it for yourself.

EXERCISE: Priming Our Heart (Tonglen)

First, settle your mind by taking three to five deep breaths, bringing each one all the way down to your belly and then gently releasing it. Then chose someone as a focus for this tonglen meditation. It could be a loved one, especially someone who is going through a difficult time; or you could chose a group of people displaced from their war-torn home and struggling to get by in a cramped refugee camp, for instance.

Now contemplate, "Just like me, they too wish to overcome suffering." On the basis of this recognition, generate a sense of concern for their well-being and the wish that they be free of pain, fear, and sorrow.

With this compassionate wish, imagine that their pain, fear, and sorrow emerge from their bodies in the form of dark clouds that enter your body . . . breathing in, they dissolve into a radiant orb of light at your heart, where they are completely extinguished. Imagine that as a result of your taking away their suffering, they become free from pain, fear, and sorrow.

While thinking of them, reinforce the thought, "Just like me, they too aspire to happiness." On the basis of this recognition, generate the wish that they find peace and joy.

As you cultivate these caring thoughts for them, and as you breathe out, imagine sending white clouds and light rays from your heart that touch them, bringing them your compassion, your joys, your good fortune, and everything that is good in you. Imagine that they find peace, strength, and happiness.

Repeat this alternating practice of taking in pain, fear, and sorrow and sending out peace, joy, and safety.

Now try to see if you can make this taking in and sending out bigger. Say, if you have just done tonglen for a loved one who is going through a difficult time, extend it to many others who might be in a similar situation. Take in . . . and send out.

You could even extend tonglen to individuals whom you consider difficult, those who wish you ill and have treated you unfairly. Contemplate that they too, just like you, do not wish to suffer; they too just wish to be happy and have peace.

Finally, if your heart feels big, extend tonglen to all beings. Imagine taking away the pain, fear, and sorrow of all beings, sending to them your loving-kindness and compassion. Remain in silence with this thought for a little while.

* * *

Tonglen is a beautiful spiritual practice, to my mind one of the most precious gifts to the world from the Tibetan tradition. It is also a spiritual practice that can be embraced by everyone, those of different faiths as well as of no faith. It's a practice that we can do anywhere, anytime, for anyone. It does not require any special place or preparation. The only thing you need is your full presence—you do need to show up to do this. Attend to the situation at hand, be with the suffering and breathe in, and as you breathe out, send your loving-kindness and compassion. Breathe in, breathe out. That's all.

Now, in the final part of the book, we shall discuss how in the wake of cultivating our kinder side, we can envision a new way of being in the world.

Part III

A New Way of Being

A New Way of Being

9

Greater Well-being

How Compassion Makes Us Healthy and Strong

If, however, we view human nature as predominantly oriented toward kindness ... we can consider ethics as an entirely natural and rational means for pursuing our innate potentials.

—The Dalai Lama

Until he extends the circle of his compassion to all living things, man will not himself find peace.

—Albert Schweitzer (1875–1965)

How does our compassion practice relate to the emerging science of well-being? Does training in compassion help promote what today's well-being researchers recognize as core dimensions of our psychological functioning?

In a series of papers, American psychologist Carol Ryff proposed a new way of conceptualizing well-being.[1] Previously, researchers had mainly concentrated on drawing distinctions between positive and negative emotions and evaluating over-all life satisfaction. The assumption was that positive emotions plus life satisfaction equals happiness, including psychological well-being. Ryff, however, compared this mainstream science of well-being with some alternative perspectives and developed an integrated model based on six "essential features of positive psychological functioning": self-acceptance, positive relations with others, autonomy, environmental mastery, purpose in life, and personal growth. Then she designed a comprehensive scale to measure each of these dimensions. Today, the new science of well-being has embraced Ryff's model.

Having *self-acceptance* means having a positive attitude toward ourselves, which is increasingly recognized as an important mental health factor. Those who score high on self-acceptance are able to accept multiple aspects of the self, both good and bad, and on the whole feel positive about their past. *Positive relation with others* pertains to social connectedness—having warm, trusting interpersonal relations in our life. Those who score high on this aspect are capable of strong empathetic connection with others, including feelings of affection and intimacy, and have concern for other people's welfare. *Autonomy* involves qualities such as self-determination, inde-pendence, and regulating our behavior from within rather than by external constraints. Highly autonomous people resist social pressures to think and act in certain ways and evaluate themselves by personal standards rather than look to others for approval. *Environmental mastery* is a kind of competence, the ability to "control a complex array of activities, make effective use of surrounding opportunities ... [and] choose or create contexts suitable to personal needs and values."[2] High *purpose in life* means having goals, a sense of directedness, and beliefs that give life meaning. Finally, on the *personal growth* dimension, we see ourselves as always growing in psychological and emotional terms (or not). People with a high personal growth score are open to new experiences, are committed to realizing their potential, and see improvement in themselves over time.

Compassion training for psychological well-being

As we saw in Chapter 7, there is no self-acceptance without self-compassion (and vice versa). In our compassion cultivation training, we treat self-acceptance, along with self-kindness, as a dimension of self-compassion. Through compassion training we learn to acknowledge, nonjudgmentally, the whole package of our reality: our vulnerability and weaknesses as well as our strengths, good fortune, and bad fortune, and we forgive ourselves for our mistakes and failings. The vast majority of CCT participants discover that relating to ourselves and our lives in this way is a profound relief. It gives us a sense of ease, of comfort in our skin (remember my grandmother in Chapter 2) that is such a tremendous release from our customary self-hating, self-punitive ways that it's not uncommon for people to get teary in class. Not surprisingly, feeling more comfortable with ourselves tends to improve our interactions with others too.

Indeed, compassion training contributes to positive relations with others, as we become more aware and appreciative of the important people in our life through consciously wishing them happiness and freedom from suffering and misfortune. Family members of the military veterans who participated in an accelerated six-week course as part of their residential treatment for PTSD have noticed the effects. Spouses, in particular, tell us how compassion training has improved the quality of their home life, as the participants returned with greater sensitivity to their spouses' feelings and needs and a renewed ability to connect with their loved ones. And expanding our circle of concern (Chapter 8) leads to *more* positive relations with *more* others.

A middle-aged doctor had decided to do compassion training because he had lost the spark in his work. As a result of the CCT course, he said, he changed the way he greeted, listened to, and interacted with his patients. One day one of his patients, an older woman, asked him if he was "in love or something," because he was acting "so different, so happy." "Or something" was that, as he told his CCT class, he felt a much stronger connection with his patients and was happy again with his work. (One might say he was "in loving-kindness.") He also talked to his CCT instructors about offering the training to other members of the hospital staff, since it had had such a powerful effect on him.[3]

The effect of compassion training on autonomy, the third dimension of psychological well-being, might be less direct. Still, making compassion part of our conscious intention as well as our basic motivation system (Chapter 4) gives us an internal compass to rely on—principles to inform our attitudes and guide our thoughts, feelings, and behavior instead of being swayed by other people's whims and societal norms.

Environmental mastery essentially relates to our sense of control. Clearly, being too obsessed with control will detract rather than contribute to our well-being, insofar as many aspects of our life will always remain outside our personal control, but research increasingly shows that some sense of control is crucial for psychological health. A simple experiment conducted with elderly people at an assisted-living residence found an amazing correlation between longevity and their sense of control. Researchers gave each of the residents a houseplant. One group had responsibility for their plants' care, while the other group was told that a member of staff would look after their plants for them. The researchers found that, about six months later, twice as many residents in the low-responsibility group had died—30 percent versus 15 percent in the high-responsibility group.[4] We can think of the plant care in this experiment as a metaphor for compassion practice: We take responsibility for taking care of ourselves, others, and the world in which we live.

As we saw in Chapter 1, compassion enhances our sense of purpose in life, and some evidence suggests that a sense of purpose is correlated to physical health and longevity. In the first place, signing up for compassion training is a purpose in itself. Then, as our practice deepens over time and our sense of connection with others along with it, we learn to take joy in bringing benefit to others. We see that our existence matters, and this inspires us to do what we can to make our existence as meaningful as possible.

Finally, compassion training is all about personal growth, the sixth dimension of psychological well-being. A conscious effort to transform our perspective on life and change the way we relate to ourselves and others as fellow human beings—in short, being in a conscious, committed process of growing—

will necessarily make us more aware of ourselves as growing beings who see life in terms of growth.

There is no doubt in my mind that if Ryff's six dimensions capture the essential features of our psychological well-being, compassion cultivation can be a powerful method for promoting it, in all its multifaceted complexity.

A compassionate mind is a resilient mind

Perhaps the greatest mental health benefit of compassion training is that it makes us more resilient. Researchers of resilience, from the field of child development as well as studies of widows coping with the loss of a spouse, have identified two critical aspects. One is called *ego-resiliency*, defined as "the capacity to overcome, steer through, and bounce back from adversity," and the other is *hardiness*, or the ability to view difficulty as a challenge rather than a threat, to commit to it rather than feel alienated by it, with a sense of control rather than powerlessness.[5]

Longitudinal studies demonstrate that children who score high in resilience are found to be "confident, perceptive, insightful, and are able to form warm and open relationships with others." In contrast, "ego-brittle" children "exhibit behavioral problems, depressive symptoms, and higher levels of drug use in adolescence." Studies also show greater ego-resiliency to be associated with quicker cardiovascular recovery in adults following a lab-induced stressful event, as well as with lower depressive symptoms among Americans who witnessed the September 11 terrorist attack in New York.[6]

The Dalai Lama often tells the remarkable story of an ordinary monk who was a member of His Holiness's personal monastery in Tibet. Unable to escape to India in 1959 with the Dalai Lama, Lopon-la remained behind in Lhasa. In the wake of the Cultural Revolution, however, he was sent to a Chinese labor camp and prison in Tibet, where he remained for eighteen years. In the early 1980s, during a period of policy relaxation inside Tibet, Lopon-la was able to come to India, where he rejoined the Namgyal Monastery. As a senior member of the monastery, occasionally he would spend time with the Dalai Lama. During one casual conversation, the Dalai Lama says, Lopon-la remarked that he faced grave dangers on one or two occasions during his prison years. Thinking that he was speaking about some kind of threat to his life, the Dalai Lama asked what kind of danger he had faced. To this, the monk replied, "The danger of losing my compassion toward the Chinese." This is resilience par excellence.

Lopon-la knew that physically there was nothing much he could do to change his situation. His daily routine was in others' hands. But he knew that he was in charge of his mind. Despite all the hardships of prison life, Lopon-la continued his spiritual practices, including generating compassion for all beings, including perpetrators of harm. He practiced generating feelings of concern for the way ignorance and circumstances had led them to do things that are ultimately damaging even to themselves. From a conventional point of view, Lopon-la's concerns about losing compassion for the Chinese might seem silly or even self-destructive. But his commitment to compassion helped him retain his sanity and not give in to bitterness or despair. I have met Lopon-la on numerous occasions. He is a tall, skinny monk with a gentle demeanor. Except for a slight hunch, a consequence possibly of having to carry so many sacks of earth on his back while in the labor camp, he seems to have come out of his difficult experience unscathed.

In my own life, I find the following rather stoic lines from Shantideva helpful:

> *If something can be done about it,*
> *what need is there for dejection?*
> *And if nothing can be done about it,*
> *what use is there for being dejected?*[7]

I call this Shantideva's "No need, no use principle." I am aware that many of the problems we face in our life are far too complex to be slotted neatly into two trays labeled "solvable" and "unsolvable." Often, the solutions to our problems require the cooperation and goodwill of other people. Even then, there is a lot we can do ourselves to invite the help we need. In any case, I try to do the best I can and then move on. It's the constant worrying, and carrying the problem on our back—actually, in our head—that makes things stressful. This is what weighs us down. When it's obvious there is nothing we can do about the situation, we need to have the wisdom to accept this and let go. This same wisdom is echoed in the well-known serenity prayer from the Christian tradition:

> *God, give me the grace to accept with serenity*
> *the things that cannot be changed,*
> *courage to change the things*
> *which should be changed,*

and the wisdom to distinguish
the one from the other.

I am partial to the words of Shantideva, for in my early monastic years I had the opportunity to memorize his famed *The Way of the Bodhisattva*. This spiritual classic in verse is the author's vision of the entire career of a person living according to the dictates of altruism, a life dedicated to the welfare of all beings. Part of my fondness comes from how I came to memorize the text. It was in 1973 in South India, where the small monastery I was a member of had moved to a Tibetan agricultural settlement near the Indian town of Hunsur. As part of an experiment for cooperative farming, one year white sorghum was planted in the fields. When the crops began to mature toward the end of summer, the fields had to be protected against birds, and the monastery sent us, the young monks, to do this. It was thus, roaming the fields of sorghum, every now and then making noises to chase away swarms of birds, that I memorized Shantideva's text. To this day, I take spiritual solace from this book and still recite with joy important verses by heart.

One of the ways we grow in resilience through compassion training is that it teaches us to see ourselves in the context of our relationship with others rather than in isolation. When we define a self-concept primarily in terms of self-interest, we become trapped within the narrow vision of our own personal concerns, plagued by cycles of hope and fear. Excessive self-preoccupation makes our mind brittle, hypersensitive to the slightest thing that might be perceived as a threat. Tibetan mind-training teachers suggest that excessive self-focus is like carrying around a large target that can easily get hit. The more excessive our self-preoccupation, the greater our vulnerability to feelings of slight and hurt.

In contrast, a compassionate mind-set is necessarily less self-preoccupied, more at ease, less inhibited. It's no exaggeration to say that through connection with others, we become free. When the ego is resilient, there's no need to put up walls and put on facades to protect it. We can stop hiding and just be. True, sometimes very kind people do get hurt and don't recover easily. They may be more sensitive to others' suffering, and perhaps *too* focused on other people's well-being. Here, it's helpful to recall the distinction we drew earlier between empathy and compassion. Empathy is critical to elicit our compassion, but if we get stuck in the empathy zone (of emotional resonance) it can be draining and lead to feelings of powerlessness and burnout. Compassion, by contrast, is a more empowered state in which we put our energy into wishing that others be free of suffering, and wanting to do something about it. What we need, at least for most of us ordinary souls, is a healthy balance between focusing on ourselves and focusing on others. This way, we do not fall into either of the two extremes of excessive self-preoccupation or obsessive caregiving. In compassion training we practice exactly this kind of balance.

Compassion training and emotion regulation

A randomized controlled study on the effects of CCT found a robust impact on emotion regulation.[8] Emotion regulation is a growing area of scientific research, in which findings have underscored how important it is to our mental and physical

health, social functioning, relationships, and work performance. Problems with emotion regulation have been associated
with unhappiness, excessive worry, and increased stress.

Actually, emotion regulation is something we do naturally;
positive and negative emotions have been arising all our lives,
and we have had to figure out ways to deal with them. A pioneer in the field, Stanford psychologist James Gross, defines
emotion regulation as "processes by which individuals influence which emotions they have, when they have them, and
how they experience or express these emotions."[9] Typical
strategies include *suppressing expression* of our emotions—for
example, keeping an emotional poker face and not showing
when we feel hurt; *reappraising* an emotional situation to give
it a more positive meaning; *distracting* ourselves with positive
or neutral activities, as in the proverbial "cold shower"; and
detachment, a form of emotional suppression that distances us
from our feelings. (Deliberately suppressing our emotions is a
form of denial response. It is very different from the distance
or disengagement *with acceptance* of meta-awareness in mindfulness.) Of these, suppressing expression of our emotions has
been "associated with increased stress related symptoms, negative emotion, depression, and anxiety, as well as decreased
positive affect and life satisfaction."[10]

Of course, not all expressions of emotion are healthy or
helpful. Recall the ex-soldier in Chapter 8 who had expressed
his anger by verbally and even physically attacking people.
Regulation, rather than suppression or unchecked expression, is the key.

To assess compassion training's effect on emotion regulation, researchers in the Stanford study used the standard

Emotion Regulation Questionnaire, designed to assess people's habitual use of two dominant emotion regulation strategies, cognitive reappraisal and expressive suppression.[11] Researchers found that a decrease in emotional suppression was significantly correlated with the amount of compassion practice that participants undertook as part of their daily homework. This comes as no surprise, since CCT encourages consciously being with our suffering, open expressions of concern, and cultivating warm-heartedness—the opposite of emotional suppression.

Emotion regulation certainly has an interactive side, and not only in the end results of how our expression or withholding affects others. Social creatures that we are, we naturally turn to others to help us regulate our emotions. In distress we instinctively seek comfort from others, especially from our loved ones. There is nothing like the hug of a loved one to calm us down, a caring ear to take the edge off of our frustrations, a smile to reassure us when we feel anxious. By deepening connection with others, especially loved ones, and by re-forming secure attachments, especially through self-compassion practice, compassion training has the potential to change how we habitually regulate our emotions.

I must admit that hugging is one area in which, as a former Tibetan monk married to a French Canadian, I had to go through basic training. Traditionally in Tibet, parents are physically very close and affectionate with their young children. Children sleep with their parents at night and often get carried on their mother's back during the day, snug inside a shawl wrapped securely around mother and child. However, after a certain age—usually in our early teens—it isn't the custom to be hugged on a regular basis. People hug each other only in special circumstances—when someone is distraught, or is leaving for a trip, or returns after a long separation, for example. Then, for a monk, as I was during most of my early life, physical contact was particularly limited, so I developed an instinctive reticence when it came to embracing someone else. This was perfectly fine when I was single. However, when my future wife, Sophie, came into my life, things had to change in that department. She once bought a book called *The Little Book of Hugs* and left it in our bathroom. It turned out to be quite helpful.

Anchoring our personal ethics

When we make compassion part of our basic motivation system (Chapter 4) we forge a solid anchor to ground our values and our personal ethics. One thing most scientists of human behavior agree on: Whether we like it or not, as human beings we are inescapably moral creatures. As rational and emotional beings it's no wonder we are also moral creatures, constantly evaluating the world around us and adjusting our responses according to our values, attitudes, and goals. How we make these evaluations and the considerations we bring to bear on them is what I mean by ethics here.

As social animals our well-being is intertwined with that of others. We don't get very far in our fundamental drive to seek happiness and alleviate suffering without other people. Our ethics guide us to maintain a balance between our very natural pursuit of well-being for ourselves and our responsibility for the well-being of others, our fellow creatures who share the same basic aspiration and have an equal right to pursue its fulfillment. Ethics is what helps us negotiate this shared moral universe. It's no surprise, therefore, that some form of the Golden Rule (Do unto others as you would have them do unto you) lies at the heart of all major systems of ethics, whether religious or secular humanistic. In Buddhist thought, for example, an ethical act is defined as one that involves refraining from actual harm toward others or from sources of such harm. And the gravity of unethical behavior is determined in accordance with the degree of harm caused, with taking life as the most severe. Inversely, proactively doing good has greater ethical value than simply avoiding harm, with altruistic deeds valued highest. In Buddhist thought, one thus speaks of the ethic of restraint, the ethic of virtue, and the ethic of altruism.

Current scientific research on the evolution of morality suggests that we might share core moral sentiments across cultures, languages, and ethnicities. Some argue that this sharing extends even to our nonhuman primate cousins. Darwin himself seems to have held a version of this view. Some proponents of natural human morality suggest that as human beings, we possess a kind of innate "moral grammar," akin to the theory of universal grammar proposed by the linguist Noam Chomsky.[12] Just as this "innate grammar"—our inborn ability to learn grammar, which is hardwired into our brain—gets expressed in specific ways with exposure to specific linguistic communities, our natural "moral grammar" manifests according to the social and cultural communities we're raised in. So, each one of us acquires a set of values, perspectives, and attitudes via the society in which we grew up. These are our personal ethics.

In the past, many societies were more homogeneous than they are today—especially with respect to ethnicity, religion, and language—and more people shared values within a given society as a result. With secularization and exposure to a plurality of value systems—two important consequences of modernity, in fact—there is little that underpins common values within a given society beyond adherence to the laws of the land. When it comes to morality, we are left to our own devices to make sense of how we relate to others and the world around us. The question for our secular and pluralistic time is this: Where do we anchor our ethics?

In my own case, my wife and I agreed that we would raise our children within the value system we share as Buddhists. Our standpoint on this was quite simple. Children absorb all sorts of attitudes and values anyway, through a host of influences—parents, schools, peers, and the larger society, especially via media—each exerting an impact on their moral character. Given this complex contemporary reality, it's important for parents to teach their children well, to impart our most cherished spiritual and ethical values. This is especially critical during the early period, when we as parents are the primary frame of reference for our children.

Compassion can be both the foundation and the organizing principle of our moral house, bringing clarity to our ethical vision. It will help us set priorities and decide between competing values, and provide us with a simple criterion to determine the bottom line when we are confronted with an ethical challenge. With compassion as our fundamental value, we will be motivated by concern for others' welfare, our actions guided by the intention to help others, and the sight of others' happiness will bring us joy.

Compassion is part of the innate disposition we share as humans. If we embrace it and nurture it, compassion can offer a universal basis for the ethics that define us, together, as moral beings.

The Dalai Lama, for example, has dedicated a large part of his efforts to promoting exactly this message, that compassion can be the foundation for "universal secular ethics." His Holiness makes a powerful case for such a perspective on ethics, especially in his book *Ethics for the New Millennium* and its sequel, *Beyond Religion*.[13] A central premise of the Dalai Lama's argument is that although basic human values such as compassion, love, kindness, forgiveness, and sense of responsibility may be promoted by religion, in themselves they are independent of religious faith. They are universal values grounded in something fundamental to our human condition: our need for connection with others, our aspiration to happiness, and our instinctive desire to avoid suffering. In brief, these values are expressions of our basic empathetic nature. Hence compassion, defined in its essence as a sense of concern for others' well-being, holds the promise of grounding our shared ethics, without recourse to any particular religious or metaphysical creed. The cultivation of compassion, therefore, can also have huge societal and global implications. Imagine what our world would be like if each one of us made compassion the organizing principle of our life.

10

More Courage, Less Stress, Greater Freedom

Making Compassion Our Basic Stance

Moral excellence comes about as a result of habit ...
We become just by doing just acts, temperate by doing tem-
*   perate acts,*
brave by doing brave acts.

—Aristotle (*Nicomachean Ethics*, Book II)

Keep your actions positive, because your actions become your
*   habits.*
Keep your habits positive, because your habits become your
*   values.*
Keep your values positive, because your values become your des-
*   tiny.*

—Gandhi (1869–1948)

Can we make a habit of compassion and altruism by setting (and resetting, and resetting) our intention to do so, and practicing (and practicing, and practicing)? Can training our heart and mind turn compassion into a subconscious, automatic process of so-called fast thinking, so that we instinctively respond to life this way? Can compassion become more than fleeting feelings—a way of seeing and being in the world?

In his influential book *Thinking, Fast and Slow*, Nobel Prize-winning economist and psychologist Daniel Kahneman made famous two different thought-forming systems in our brain.[1] What he calls the *fast system* is associated primarily with our emotions and tends to be automatic, operating below the surface of our consciousness. The *slow system* involves effortful, conscious, rational functioning. We tend to rely on the fast system more in our decision making in everyday life. From the evolutionary point of view, this makes perfect sense. The more automatic system enables us to process information faster, facilitating our most efficient response to the needs of a given situation. This system gets its speed from associating new information with existing patterns of thought, feeling, and behavior rather than creating new responses for every new situation. In other words, it reuses behavior patterns that we've internalized since they have proven to be useful in the past. With the fast system, we don't have to reinvent the wheel. Applying this theory, Kahneman revolutionized our understanding of how we make judgments and decisions, and in the process offered a compelling account of our biases as well.

Coming on the heels of Kahneman's book, journalist Charles Duhigg's *The Power of Habit* brought to popular awareness important findings in science on how habits form and how they motivate human behavior. Duhigg offered an account of how Kahneman's so-called fast thinking works. Scientists call the process by which our "brain converts a sequence of actions into an automatic routine" chunking. They believe that chunking is the root of habits. The neurobiological phenomenon of chunking has a crucial evolutionary function, as our brain is constantly looking for ways to save effort. When a habit emerges, the brain stops working hard on that particular task and conserves its finite energy to focus on other matters. Duhigg sums up the key message of his book: "At one point, we all consciously decided how much to eat and what to focus on when we go to the office, how often to have a drink or when to go for a jog. Then we stopped making a choice, and the behavior became automatic. It's a natural consequence of our neurobiology. And by understanding how it happens, you can rebuild those patterns in whichever way you choose."[2]

In light of what we know today from psychology and neuroscience, the answer to the questions at the start of this chapter has to be yes. Buddhist tradition, for one, has consistently advocated the transformational value of practices aimed at cultivating our compassion. If we have learned anything from contemporary neuroscience, it's that our brain is highly amenable to change in response to new experience. Not only do new synaptic connections form; new neurons are created through our interactions with our environment. The birth of new neurons is called *neurogenesis*, and our brain's ability to change throughout our lives is more generally known as *neuroplasticity*.[3] New findings even suggest *epigenetic* effects in the brain—meaning genetic changes resulting from environmental influence—as a result of experience, which endure over a lifetime and, in some cases, can even be passed on to our offspring.

Compassion in everyday life

When we make a habit of compassion in our everyday lives through regular practice and action, we live with more courage, less stress, and greater freedom. In time, we will automatically see ourselves and the world in terms of inter-connectedness. Our default position toward other people will be as fellow humans rather than as sources of antagonism and threat. Our new, other-oriented habits will free us from the old habits of self-judgment, self-protection, and worrying about ourselves. Our relationships, from chance interactions with strangers to our intimate connections with our closest family and friends, will be permeated with a sense of openness and kindness rooted in the understanding of our fundamental human condition—our shared needs, vulnerability, and basic aspiration for happiness. We will habitually respond to all people's suffering and needs with compassion, unprejudiced by who they are in relation to us. Even when it comes to a diffi-cult person who causes us problems, we will not lose sight of the basic fact: *Just like me, he too is a fellow human who aspires to happiness and does not wish to suffer.* These thoughts will have entered our fast system. Our actions too will reflect our deep, even cellular knowledge of the impact we have on others. Our habit of kindness will be reinforced over and over by the joy we take in being kind to others and seeing them happy. Being helpful will be our new normal. We will come to embody com-passion, not just admire it as an ideal. We will learn to live it through our thoughts, feelings, and behavior. In short, making a habit of compassion will transform our lives.

Being compassionate does not make us timid or tolerant of injustice. On a societal level, in fact, a truly compassionate response to injustice stems from a sense of strong moral outrage—a form of anger, but a constructive one. It was moral outrage that spurred Mahatma Gandhi to lead the Indian people to freedom from British Colonial rule, drove Abraham Lincoln in his campaign against slavery, led Rosa Parks to courageously defy bus segregation one cold December morning in Montgomery, Alabama, and moved Nelson Mandela to lead a lifelong campaign against the apartheid system. Thanks to their strong sense of moral outrage and courage, today our world is a better place. What sustains the amazing courage of the young Pakistani activist Malala Yousafzai is her moral outrage at the injustice of the Taliban's ban on the education of girls. At the root of their moral outrage: a deep concern for the welfare of others, especially the weak and the downtrodden.

A theory of personal transformation

Classical Buddhist psychology recognizes the important role of habit formation in personal transformation and change, and traditional Buddhist compassion practices reflect this understanding. The original Sanskrit word for meditation, *bhavana*, connotes "cultivation," while its Tibetan equivalent, *gom*, carries the notion of developing "familiarity." Through repetition over time, we come to internalize and embody a certain way of seeing, feeling, and being in the world. Even tasks that initially require deliberate conscious effort can eventually become effortless and spontaneous. This, in essence, is what happens when we gain expertise over something.

We know from personal experience how, through practice, what seemed effortful initially can become effortless. When we first learn to ride a bike, it's mighty hard to balance, pedal, and stay on the road on two narrow moving wheels! I had even greater difficulty learning how to drive. By then I was already in my early thirties. As I was living in a village outside Cambridge (friends had generously lent me a cottage free of rent on their property), I desperately needed to drive to get around. As a monk in India, I had never learned to ride or drive anything more challenging than a bicycle, so the sensation of being in charge of something powered by a motor was completely alien and quite terrifying. I learned to drive a manual transmission with the driving instructor drumming his mantra, "MSM—mirror, signal and maneuver," into me at literally every turn. The conscious attention required for every detail—checking the mirrors, not forgetting to indicate, shifting gears by depressing the clutch at the right time—required constant effort. I knew that at some point driving would become effortless, but at the time it was impossible to imagine how this could happen. I failed my first driving test, which shook me a little because I really wanted to be able to drive. Today, it is hard for me to imagine driving being so hard!

Modern cognitive psychology distinguishes between declarative and procedural knowledge. The first relates to knowledge *about*, while the second has to do with the knowledge of *how*, acquired primarily through actual performance of the task involved. Broadly, one could say that declarative knowledge is cognitive and has to do with facts, while procedural knowledge is embodied knowledge. Knowing how to drive is procedural knowledge, while the knowledge that a turbo engine gives greater acceleration is declarative. In compassion training, we aim not merely to know about compassion, but more important, for compassion and altruism to become embodied knowledge and part of our character.

Buddhist psychology has a theory about how this happens based on three levels of understanding: First is understanding *derived through hearing*, at which stage our understanding remains primarily verbal, tied to words and laden with assumptions. Our knowledge at this stage is nothing but an informed assumption. However, as we continue to contemplate that knowledge, we reach the second level, called understanding *derived through critical reflection*. At this stage, our knowledge becomes intellectually rigorous, well processed, integrated into our larger body of knowledge, and supported by conviction. Finally, we reach the level of understanding *derived through meditative experience*, which results from a long process of internalizing our understanding to the point that it becomes part of our basic mental landscape. It's at this final stage that our knowledge becomes effortless, integrated, and experiential. What was previously a deliberate cognitive understanding has transformed into an embodied spontaneous knowledge.

We might study, say, the interdependent nature of things, a key concept in Buddhism. This is the idea that everything comes into being as a consequence of multiple causes and conditions, and how every action or event has effects across time as well as space. Initially, our understanding will come from readings and teachings. It will necessarily be somewhat superficial and tied closely to words. However, with reflection on this idea of interdependence, analyzing it and relating the concept to our own experience, eventually a deeper sense of conviction arises in us. We apply our new awareness to our everyday life so that we become less fixated and less categorical in our judgment. We learn to relate to situations, especially adverse ones, with a greater degree of tolerance and composure, and we notice the effects. Now, in order to radically impact our psyche and behavior, we must integrate the knowledge into the very fabric of our mind-set. This third level of understanding is thought to arise only by internalizing our insight through a prolonged, repetitive process of disciplined inner reflection; in other words, meditation.

We can apply this same model to compassion. An early Buddhist text compares the early stages of learning compassion to tasting the bark of sugarcane, while the advanced, experiential compassion is like eating the real thing, the sugar of the sugarcane. In the first stage, our compassion for all beings remains effortful, imagined, and imitated. With contemplation and practice our compassion becomes effortless, spontaneously arising in response to the needs of others without any deliberate thought on our part.

Seeing, feeling, and acting

As we have seen, the relationship between perception, experience, and action is complex, cyclical, and bidirectional. That is to say, our emotions inform our thoughts as well as our behavior, while our behavior reshapes our emotional life and informs our perceptions and attitudes at the same time. These dynamics are particularly evident in the psychology of desire, craving, and compulsive behavior. In Buddhist thought, the first link in the chain is described as *contact*—namely, coming into contact with the thing, which gives rise to an *experience* that manifests as either pleasurable or not pleasurable. This affective or emotional response then comes to define our memory of the thing, so that the next time we come into contact with it, even before experiencing it, we start to fantasize about it, making the thing seem far more important and attractive, or unattractive, to us than was previously the case. This kind of engagement with the object leads to *craving*, wanting to possess what we do not have, believing that somehow having it will lead to relief or happiness. Unchecked craving takes on a life of its own, as we reach automatically and repetitively for the object of our desire, leading to further craving.

For better or worse, many of our perspectives on the world—our perceptions, thoughts, attitudes, and values—are shaped by our environment, especially our family and the culture we grew up with. Cognitive science tells us how even our basic perceptual apparatus, which we take to be so fundamental and neutral, is influenced by our upbringing. Human history is replete with examples of how societal attitudes bias people's perceptions, which are felt to be universal and true. For example, many people in the premodern West, including devout Christians, saw slavery as completely unproblematic.

So societal prejudices create blind spots that we need to be outside the box to recognize. In India, some orthodox Hindus still view the *Dalits*, the so-called "untouchables," as intrinsically inferior and avoid any direct contact with them. Many fundamentalist Islamists view nonbelievers, or *kafirs*, to be intrinsically unclean and not worthy of respect and concern. In Tibetan culture, I was surprised to learn of the prejudice in certain regions of central Tibet against those from hereditary families of butchers and smiths. I saw firsthand how this prejudice manifests in practice. The small monastery I was a member of when I was in my teens was part of a Tibetan colony in southern India, about fifty kilometers west of the city of Mysore. During a harvest party, a tent was pitched at the crossroads at the center of the camp. Inside on a table were two pots, one large and one small, filled with fermented millet soaked with water. This is the homemade beer called *chang*, sipped through straws inserted into the fermented millet. The smaller pot, I found out, was for those few who were from the "inferior" class of smiths' and butchers' parentage.

The good news is, no matter how deeply rooted such acquired biases may be, we can change them. The Dalai Lama often quotes his late friend Carl von Weizsäcker, a well-known German quantum physicist who said that when he was growing up, the French were the enemy in every German's eye and vice versa. By the end of the twentieth century this had completely changed, with Germany and France becoming the two closest allies in the European Union. Contemporary science also tells us that we can replace an old worldview with new ways of seeing the world, and old habits with new. This, in essence, is what education is about. This is also what compassion training is all about: *learning to see, feel, and be in a new way that is more in touch with our better self.* An important part of this transformational process is actually a kind of unlearning of habitual patterns that are not constructive to our own or others' well-being. Some of these patterns might have roots in early childhood, making them less flexible. But even here, I believe that sustained compassion practices can effect real change. I believe it because I have seen it.

At sixty-nine, Susan had been depressed most of her adult life.[4] Her mother was clinically depressed when Susan was born, so Susan had rarely been held as a baby. As a child, Susan's entire life had been shaped around her mother's depression. Over time she learned how to wall off the trauma of her youth. This changed when Susan participated in an eight-week compassion training course. From about the midpoint of the course, she talked about feeling happier than she ever had before, and about how her friends said that she was like a different person. Apparently, that change continued as Susan faced her own suffering, her mother's suffering, and how their suffering connected Susan to all of humanity. She had always loved music, but didn't feel she deserved the joy of it. Because of her experience in the course, not only did she throw herself back into her music; she applied for and won a fellowship to study music over the summer. She was amazed, and thrilled, and wanted her compassion training instructor to know. Even deep-seated psychological ruts can be undone and replaced by more constructive habits. It's interesting—many stories of personal transformation, like Susan's, show how a seemingly small shift in one area opens up a whole cascade of changes.

A perceptual shift can change how we actually feel

So, a key insight emerges from both classical Buddhist psychology and contemporary cognitive science, as we saw briefly in Chapter 4 as well: There is an intimate connection between our perceptions and emotions.[5] In the Buddhist view, feeling permeates every cognitive event, even a seemingly neutral one like solving a crossword puzzle. Contemporary cognitive science also suggests that by shaping the way we see ourselves and the world around us we reshape how we experience ourselves and the world. Similarly, by changing the way we feel about ourselves, about others, and about the world, we reshape the way we perceive ourselves, others, and the world we live in.

Sometimes, the impact on our feeling from a changed perception can be instantaneous. I experienced this in a powerful way when I was fifteen. During my years, from age eight to eleven, at the refugee boarding school in Shimla, a housemother had for some reason treated me unkindly. She and her husband looked after about thirty of us in one of the boys' dormitories at the school. I admit I was rather precocious and quite full of myself, but nothing could justify the way she treated some of us. When we took our Sunday showers in a communal bathroom, she would single out a few of us to soap up first, scrubbed us hard with dry coconut grass, and made us wait our turn to be rinsed last. We were not allowed to rinse ourselves and had to wait while our eyes burned with soap. Over the winter break one year, as my mother had died and my father was ill, I had to stay at school along with those children who were either orphans or whose parents were too poor to pay for travel costs. So I spent one snowy Shimla winter in flip-flops; she told me that I had already used my allotted pair of shoes for the year. That's when I learned that when your feet are cold it's extremely difficult to keep your body warm.

After I left school, when I was eleven, to join the monastery, I used to wonder how I might react if I ever came face-to-face with this woman again. Then it happened. I was fifteen and familiar with many stories of the hardships of displacement in the wake of the Tibetans' escape to India. I saw my former housemother carrying a load of firewood on her back, with a shovel on top, walking down the road in the scorching heat of a South Indian summer. It turned out she and her family had joined the same resettlement camp where my monastery had moved. She looked small, sweaty, and darkened by the sun, with struggle sketched on her forehead in deep wrinkles. At the sight of her, instead of resentment I felt sorry for her pain. I realized that although I had suffered her mistreatment, being a young child I was also shielded from the painful memories of total displacement she must have experienced, having lost everything only a few years before: her country, her home, and the familiar world she had left behind to come into exile in India. There she was, in North India, looking after more than thirty children, none of them her own. Confronted with such toil, it's entirely human to react harshly to those children who were defiant or self-entitled. Perhaps there was nothing personal in her treatment of me; I just happened to be the trigger that unfortunately brought out her more unpleasant side. The next time I met her, about a month later, I went over and introduced myself. At first, she didn't recognize me, but when she did she said, "Yes, you were a good friend to my daughter at the school." The simple recognition of her vulnerability as a fellow human completely changed the way I felt about her.

The goal of compassion training is simply this: to temper

our heart and mind in such a way that we instinctively relate to ourselves and others with awareness of our needs and the basic vulnerability that unites us as humans.

A way of being in the world

In Buddhism there is the ideal of the bodhisattva, a person who has chosen to live his or her life according to the principle of universal compassion—an undifferentiated sense of concern for the well-being of all beings. This has always inspired me. How does the bodhisattva live this ideal in actual practice? He or she takes a vow to live within the framework of the practice of the *six perfections*: generosity, ethical virtue, forbearance, joyful perseverance, concentration, and wisdom. Although the context of this book is secular and thus very different, this framework of the six perfections can be a useful guide to someone who aspires to live his or her life in tune with the principle of compassion, even in the secular world.

It's no surprise that classical Buddhism chose *generosity* to be the first practical translation of the principle of compassion. In the world's other great spiritual traditions too, the virtue of generosity or charity (in Christianity) and *zakat* (in Islam) is highly extolled as a way of honoring the divinity. Today's researchers on human behavior use giving as a measure of an individual's altruism. The meaning of generosity, however, should not be narrowly confined to the charitable giving of material things. Giving your attention, time, and skill to contribute to others' welfare are all acts of generosity. So too are giving spiritual counsel, psychological comfort and peace, and a feeling of safety and security. Those who are fortunate to possess material resources can give as a way of expressing their basic compassionate spirit. The point is to be generous not just in action but also in spirit and heart. Classical Buddhist texts speak of three forms of giving: giving of material needs, giving freedom from fear—making people feel safe—and giving spiritual counsel. In contemporary terms, the first relates to our conventional charitable giving, while the second would include much of the work of the caregiving professions, such as nursing, medicine, therapy, firefighting, and policing, with teaching and counseling as examples of the third category.

The second of the six perfections, *ethical virtue*, is summed up in this simple principle: *Help others if you can; if not, at least refrain from harming them.* If we take this seriously, we need to be conscious of the consequences of our actions not just on others but also on the natural environment. Ethics not only relates to acts of restraint; it also includes virtue, in which we consciously engage in virtuous and altruistic deeds.

The third, *forbearance*, refers to a particular way of dealing with events, especially those that challenge us adversely. Instead of giving in to anger, hostility, and impatience, we choose understanding, kindness, and patience as the basis of our response. There are three types of forbearance identified in classical Buddhist texts:[6] forbearance in the form of equanimity toward those who cause us harm, forbearance as voluntary acceptance of hardships in the pursuit of higher purpose, and forbearance born from understanding the deeper nature of reality. We know from our own experience that the more we care for someone, the more we can exercise patience with that person—including ourselves. The entire family of mental qualities related to forbearance—patience, understanding, and forgiveness—are expressions of kindness and compassion.

The fourth is *joyful perseverance*, which goes beyond an initial effort to maintaining joy and enthusiasm in our pursuit of altruism. This virtue depends on sustaining motivation—in other words, determination. Several factors are important here. One is being convinced of the nobility of our pursuit; another is being prepared, recognizing that there are bound to be challenges involved. In Buddhist texts, adopting an attitude of joyful perseverance at the outset is compared to putting on armor so that our motivation and determination are not easily undermined by adversity and setbacks. According to these texts, in practice, four forces promote joyful effort: a deep sense of conviction in the value of our task, steadfastness in the pursuit, joy and enthusiasm, and the ability to let go—knowing when to relax our efforts so that we don't get burned out.

The fifth of the six perfections, *concentration*, relates primarily to the quality of focus and attention we bring to our engagement. The more attention we give to compassion and altruism, the less vulnerable we'll be to distraction; for example, by self-centered rumination. With this virtue of concentration, we gain a degree of mastery over our mind so that we can direct it toward the goals and pursuits that we truly value.

Finally, there is *wisdom*, which enables us to deepen our compassion, and more important, helps translate it into wise acts that are in tune with reality. This final factor—wisdom, or insight—is considered so crucial that it's like the eye that allows the other five virtues to see. In fact, the perfect union of wisdom and compassion is envisioned as the true awakening of the Buddha. Irrespective of its traditional Buddhist roots, the cultivation and pursuit of these six virtues offers a useful framework for those of us who take compassion seriously to guide our way of life. I, for one, find it helpful as I strive to live in accordance with the ideal of compassion, especially in our increasingly globalized, competitive, and fast-paced world.

From a feeling to our very way of being

Throughout these pages we have repeatedly acknowledged how we are, by very nature, empathetic creatures; how we humans have an amazing ability to connect with others, to get into other people's shoes and minds. In the face of someone else's needs and pain, we instinctively respond with kindness, understanding, and care. We do not need religion or schooling to teach us this. Each of us instinctively longs for connection with others. We crave others' affection, their affirmation, and their assurance. Even our experience of happiness and suffering, which defines us as sentient, is profoundly shaped by our relationship with others. These are the fundamental facts of our human condition.

This said, whether we make empathy and compassion guiding forces in our life is clearly a matter of choice, individual as well as cultural. The way we see ourselves and the world around us, the attitudes we bring to the world, the values we cherish, and the action we take all determine whether or not compassion plays an important role as an organizing principle in our life. Compassion training connects us with the kinder part of our nature. But if we're not in the habit of compassion, it will take some intention, determination, and practice to make it our default position and the organizing principle of our life.

So the goal of cultivating compassion is both ambitious and radical. It transforms our very being, and changes how we behave in the world. This is true spiritual transformation.

11

The Power of One

The Way to a More Compassionate World

All human beings are born free and equal in dignity and rights. They are endowed with reason and conscience and should act toward one another in a spirit of brotherhood.

—Universal Declaration of Human Rights, Article 1

As long as space remains,
As long as sentient beings remain,
Until then, may I too remain
And help dispel miseries of the world.

—Shantideva (eighth century)

Up to this point, we have looked at compassion mainly from the point of view of each of us as individuals. However, "no man is an island," and as we've seen, the fate of each one of us is intertwined with all the rest of us.[1] The social, political, and economic systems that make up our society impact our welfare and our day-to-day lives.

Many of us feel powerless when we think about the big

problems of the world. War, terrorism, climate change and environmental destruction, poverty and the growing gap between the rich and the poor—our problems seem so huge and complicated that we can hardly understand them, let alone solve them. Even if we have some intuition about how compassion could help, we still have no idea how to make that work. We know, for example, that being compassionate with our families is something we can do; but we have no idea what our part might be in creating, say, a more compassionate corporation. In this final chapter, we'll consider how we might break down some of these problems so that they begin to seem more manageable, and we'll identify, wherever possible, the crucial roles individuals can play in making the world a more compassionate place. In the end, no matter how complex, crowded, or messed up modern society might appear to be, it is made up of individuals just like you and me. So the practical question for each of us is this: What does it mean for me to practice compassion, not just personally, but publicly as well?

Compassion in our health care systems

It's obvious that health care is one institution in which we need to make compassion a priority, particularly in training primary health care providers. From communicating with patients and family, especially when delivering bad news, to being fully present with each patient, incorporating compassion training in formal training could change the very culture of hospitals and their patient care.

This would also give health care professionals skills to deal with the constant exposure to acute suffering and the considerable emotional impact that is part of their everyday work. Many use suppression as a coping strategy, distancing themselves and keeping "professionally" detached. However, as we saw in Chapter 9, suppression isn't good for us in the long run. On the other hand, as we have also discussed, staying open and empathetic all the time can leave us feeling overwhelmed and burned out. No matter how mentally strong we might be, there is only so much a person can take. An unregulated response can be difficult from the patient's perspective as well. Patients and their families need composure and confidence from their health care experts, not someone who appears to be an emotional wreck. But we also need our health care providers to care.

Is there a right balance between professionalism and caring? Compassion training says yes. Through compassion practice, health care providers can learn how to be fully engaged with the suffering of the patient and yet not get emotionally drained since, critically, with compassion our empathetic response is tempered by the wish to see someone become free from suffering, and we feel energized by the impulse to do something about the situation. Compassion, as I hope is clear by now, is an empowered state.

To distinguish the brain systems involved in empathy and compassion, noted empathy researcher Tania Singer sought the help of the French Buddhist monk and author Matthieu Ricard in a series of brain imaging sessions. In these fMRI sessions, Matthieu was asked to deliberately remain in a state of empathy after it had been induced through exposure to images of suffering, and not to move on to compassion. After a while he was asked to move on to compassion, wishing alleviation of that suffering for the object of his concern. Matthieu-la, as those who know him affectionately call him, reports how moving on to compassion felt like a release, a kind of joyous relief. In contrast, he said staying in empathy was exhausting.[2] Since then, Matthieu-la has become more vocal in advocating the idea that what we call "compassion fatigue" should actually be framed more accurately as "empathy fatigue," with compassion offering a way out.

Already there are health care centers that recognize compassion training as a crucial component of professional education and self-care. In San Diego, Sharp HealthCare, a major private health care association with approximately 20,000 employees, for example, has offered the Stanford CCT course since 2011. Among those who participated in the course, the preliminary results show significant positive effects on job satisfaction, interpersonal relations, and self-compassion.[3] At Stanford itself, the medical school has recently introduced CCT classes to interested student physicians. Similarly, noted Zen teacher Roshi Joan Halifax has developed a special course on compassion for physicians. Known by its acronym, GRACE (gratitude, respect, attention, compassion, and embodiment), the program is helpful especially for physicians working in terminal care.

When it comes to actual therapies, just as with mindfulness, no doubt we will see compassion training adapted for treatments for more disorders, from relapse prevention in depression to substance abuse, PTSD, social phobia, and excessive stress. Paul Gilbert's compassion focused therapy (CFT) for patients suffering from high shame and pathological negative self-judgment is just one example. Acceptance and commitment therapy (ACT), developed by Steven Hayes and others, is another, in this case incorporating aspects of self-compassion, such as nonjudgmental acceptance and a kinder attitude toward oneself. In cognitive therapies too, I imagine more integrated methods will emerge. There is also great potential for compassion training in relationship and family therapy and parenting and workplace counseling, in which constructive engagement with others depends on a healthy relationship with ourselves.

Ultimately, the very ethos of our health care systems can and must stem from compassion. Regardless of whether the system is public, as in Canada, where I live, or private, as in the United States, the main objective of health care must be how best to serve the patients, based on the premise that people seek service out of a primary need, and when they do so, most of the time, they are also at their most vulnerable. Even for private health care systems, compassion is in their long-term self-interest. It promotes positive relations between patients and health care providers, makes patients feel more assured, and is good for the reputation of the institutions themselves. In health care, compassion is a win for all stakeholders.

Re-envisioning how we educate our children

Education needs more focus on compassion too. As our world becomes ever more interconnected, our younger generation urgently needs to learn how to relate to others from the perspective of our shared humanity. If we expect our children to maintain their sanity, health, and happiness given the complexity and stress of modern life, we must equip them with cognitive and emotion regulation skills; we must teach them to manage their own minds and tend to their hearts—their own and each other's. This is what compassion training does. It's encouraging to know that, thanks to widespread respect for emotional intelligence in the wake of Daniel Goleman's influential book, *Emotional Intelligence*, many schools in North America and Europe already include social and emotional learning (SEL) in their curriculum.[4] Studies have shown that teaching children healthy emotion regulation helps them learn. A recent study of a twelve-week mindfulness-based kindness curriculum, delivered for preschool children, found robust effects on children's executive function, self-regulation, and prosocial behavior.[5]

In Montreal, where I live, there is a private French school called École Buissonnièrre, where my two daughters went for their kindergarten and primary education. In 2008, the school initiated a bold experiment to test whether, instead of merely reacting to the problem of bullying as is arises, a proactive approach to teach children certain skills pertaining to self-regulation, empathy, and peaceful conflict resolution could tangibly improve the school culture. The program, known as Ma Classe, Zone de Paix (My Class, a Peaceful Zone), is the brainchild of my wife, Sophie, who developed it on the basis of, in part, the principles of nonviolent communication (NVC).[6]

Children as young as five are taught how to check their "emotion temperature" by looking at a "thermometer," a laminated board with an image of an erupting volcano at the top, a soothing green "calm alert zone" in the middle, and an icy "cold zone" at the bottom. If, for example, six-year-old Thomas is feeling angry and agitated, he can identify with the volcano; if he is feeling uninterested and detached, he is in the cold zone. Stuck in either of these states, Thomas will not be able to connect with his fellow classmates constructively, which will make it difficult for him to play with them. So Thomas and his friends learn self-calming exercises, such as deep belly breathing and gentle rhythmic drumming on their knees, to soothe their volcano feelings. One favorite exercise is the "secret garden." Each child comes up with a visual image of a quiet, safe garden of his own, where he can feel safe, peaceful, and relaxed. Thomas and his friends would do this exercise by closing their eyes and taking a few deep breaths to settle down. They then imagine themselves in their gardens, feeling what it's like to be there. It's touching to hear from some of our daughters' friends, years later, how, as teenagers, they still go to their secret gardens when they're stressed out.

As Thomas progresses, he would expand his repertoire of emotion words to embrace a spectrum of important feelings—happy, sad, angry, afraid, safe, and so on. In the kindergarten years, the children match images of facial expressions to what they are feeling. By his second and third years at school, Thomas's emotional literacy would typically have grown to include the ability to say that he is feeling joyful, curious, frustrated, angry, lonely, disappointed, contented, worried, cautious, excited, confused, playful, surprised, relieved, and grateful.

One powerful function of the Zone de Paix program involves connecting these personal feelings with underlying universal needs. If Thomas is feeling angry and lashes out at a classmate on the playground, it may be because he feels excluded, which violates his need for inclusion. All children need safety, respect, friendship, peace, choice, personal space, rest, play, and inclusion in a community or a sense of belonging. When these needs are violated they feel threatened, which they express through emotions like anger, frustration, sadness, or fear. As NVC founder Marshall Rosenberg has put it, "Judgment, criticisms, diagnosis, and interpretations of others are all alienated expressions of our needs."[7] Thomas and his friends learn about their basic needs and practice being aware of them in real time, and you might be surprised how quickly they get it! They take turns saying, "I need x," and checking whatever they happen to choose against the question "Do all children need it?" If the answer is no, then it is not a real need. So, things like iPads can be excluded from the list quite easily. Having learned what it feels like to be angry, sad, and afraid, and also having learned to connect these negative feelings with underlying needs that are common to all, Thomas and his friends then extend this understanding to others. This conscious approach of connecting with the feelings and needs of others on the basis of his own feelings and needs helps little Thomas use his natural capacity for empathy in a constructive way.

One of the most attractive outcomes of the program from the school's perspective is an efficient system of conflict resolution, in which the children involved in the conflict are themselves the agents of resolution and the adults simply facilitate an exchange in which each child explains what the other might have felt, and more important, what might have been the underlying need of the other child that was not met. Through this process, often the children resolve their conflict and make up within one to three minutes.

At the end of the first year of this experiment, I spoke to the principal at a school celebration and thanked her for courageously offering my wife the opportunity to test her program. She said, "I must thank you for sharing her time with the school. The impact of the program has been tangible. This year, for instance, there has been around a fifty percent reduction in disciplinary cases coming to my office." Now, in the sixth year of the program, the teachers have reported a much greater feeling of connection and sense of community among themselves. When teachers feel heard, seen, and valued by their peers, students, and the school authorities, as well as by parents, this affects the entire school culture, with students being the ultimate beneficiaries.

For more than three decades now, the Dalai Lama has been calling for a fundamental rethinking of our education system. As he reminds us, modern education has its roots in medieval Europe, when religious institutions took primary responsibility for moral development. Today, in our secular society, with the public role of the Church much diminished, the time has come for our education institutions to rethink their role. Should we continue to confine the education of our children to academic development? Or should we aim to develop the whole child, brain and heart? Should we teach our children essential skills to thrive in a new world characterized, thanks to a global economy and information technology, by the increasing proximity of peoples, cultures, and religions? If the answer to these crucial questions is yes, the Dalai Lama argues that we must teach fundamental human values—the universal secular ethics I spoke of in Chapter 9 that lie at the heart of all major spiritual and ethical traditions and define us as members of the same human family—as part of our children's formal education.[8]

In 2013, the Mind and Life Institute, an organization cofounded by the Dalai Lama, took on the challenge. It has brought together experts from neuroscience and psychology as well as education to figure out what an education in secular ethics might entail. At the heart of their answer so far is the recognition that our caring instinct is the basis of our moral sentiment, and our social and ethical development is defined by the three primary modes of care: receiving care from others, extending care to others, and self-care. As someone who has been closely connected with the Mind and Life Institute since its birth in 1987, I am eager to see how this initiative might inspire change.

Whether the next and future generations rise to the complex challenges of our interconnected world depends on how we educate our children. Whether our children grow up with feelings of fellowship, a collective sense of responsibility, and hearts that care for the fate of our world is really up to us.

Caring workplace, caring economics

In many ways, the workplace is for us what school is for our children. The culture our workplace embodies and how we are treated there deeply impact our well-being. At the very least, organizations can make compassion a principle of their human resources philosophy. When employee dissatisfaction and conflict are met with empathy, concern, and understanding rather than seen as annoying complaints, employees tend to feel more loyal and committed overall. So, bringing compassion into the culture of the workplace not only helps alleviate human suffering; ultimately, it's also good for business.

For more than a decade, the University of Michigan has been home to an interesting initiative called the CompassionLab, which examines compassion in the context of organizations.[9] This collaborative study operates from the premise that organizations are "sites of everyday healing and pain" and aims to develop theoretical frameworks that would help explain how compassion can become organized and spread throughout an organization. Or, in practical terms, "What are the factors that amplify and inhibit compassion in an organization?" CompassionLab researchers have identified three interrelated factors that help organize collective compassionate response: the presence of networks of people who know each other well enough to share each other's pain; established routines within the organization for service that fosters regularity in human contact; and values such as shared humanity. Their studies also highlight the role of an organization's leader in spreading compassion; he or she must lead by compassionate example—"walk the walk"—to affect the culture of the organization. Compassion, personal integrity, humility, being open to others' perspectives yet taking responsibility to lead, all rooted in courage and a quiet confidence—these are the marks of truly great leaders.

It's one thing to call for compassion in the workplace. But is there a place for compassion in our economic systems? Is compassion at best irrelevant to or, ultimately, incompatible with our economic behavior? This is a difficult question. Nonetheless I do believe that the new wave of human psychology—recognizing that our caring and compassionate side plays a powerful motivating role in *all* human behavior—challenges some of the assumptions behind our standard economic models. We are not merely self-serving short-term-profit maximizers. It's this concept of human nature that justifies aggressive competitiveness, unchecked resource consumption, and unlimited growth.

For individuals as well as corporations, monetary gain should not be the only yardstick for success. When we define success in purely monetary terms, people hang their dignity and sense of self-respect on how much they make or acquire. In the wake of the global economic crisis of 2008, which caused so much pain to millions worldwide, people were outraged at the Wall Street culture of greed. Yes, greed was a major factor, but in some ways, it is a symptom of a deeper, systemic problem, namely our whole materialistic ethos.

Today's aggressive corporate culture, which really began to gather steam in the 1980s when the unscrupulous world of mergers and acquisitions came to be glamorized in the media, is clearly unsustainable. While the average employee's pay has barely kept pace with inflation, top executives' pay has increased exponentially. According to studies, from 1978 to 2013, chief executives' earnings in the United States increased 937 percent, while a typical employee's pay rose just over 10 percent.[10] This is a dangerous trend. Today even some economists warn that unless something changes, the developed world is set to return to the extreme income inequality of the nineteenth century, when most of the wealth was in the hands of the top 1 percent of the population.[11] Such an unequal world is not in the interest of anyone, not even the top 1 percent. Some question whether our classic economic model is fundamentally flawed, arguing that capital market theory does not take into account a world with limited, nonrenewable (or non-substitutable) natural resources, where current generations cannot be relied on to manage resources fairly or to care for the interest of future generations.

To me, it's a question of fairness, whether across current stakeholders or across generations. To ensure greater fairness in the system, we need professional economists challenging today's market orthodoxy of short-term-profit maximization, we need smart economic policies on the part of national leaders and public officials, and we all need to challenge the values that underpin unfairness in practice. Already, thanks to public pressure, companies are beginning to use environmental as well as "social responsibility" measures as part of their performance reports. Today, there are businesses in the United States and elsewhere known as B corps (benefit corporations), which seek to benefit society and the environment while making profits at the same time. For these corporations, social goals (constructive contributions to society and the planet) factor critically in their decision-making process.

This would not be the first day of economic policy that compassion has won. As societal norms change, so do our standards of acceptable economic behavior. Today, with international standards such as the Universal Declaration of Human Rights and those governing labor rights, as well as growing environmental concerns, as a society, we no longer tolerate the exploitative practices of our early industrial period. Sadly, there are still parts of the world where abusive sweatshops and dangerous work conditions exist to produce cheap products with hefty profits, but even there, the laws of the land and the society as a whole deem such practices unacceptable. (They continue through lack of political will and law enforcement to stop them.)

In today's world of instant communication and democratic online platforms such as microblogging and social media sites, businesses that ask for customers' trust must strive harder to demonstrate their trustworthiness. An organization's integrity will help it stay out of court and avoid scandalous headlines, and give its employees more reason to be dedicated and proud. Clearly, compassion can go a long way toward maintaining the highest degree of integrity.

"A very different company"

A remarkable story of a global business illustrates how a compassionate vision can be realized at the organizational level. The Camellia Group of companies was created by Gordon Fox, someone I have known and admired for a long time. Gordon is a soft-spoken man who combines the mind and the heart, rigor and sensitivity in a way that seems effortless. A longtime student of Zen and Japanese tea ceremony, he first traveled to India in 1956, at which time he fell in love with the Darjeeling region at the foothills of the Himalayas. The sight of the snow-capped Kanchenjunga peaks from the vantage point of Badamtam Tea Estate near Darjeeling has left a lasting impression for thousands of people over the years since. In these tea gardens there was a tradition handed down from generation to generation, with owners caring for the well-being of tea pickers above and beyond their job description, including their health, education, family harmony, and long-term employment. Gordon happened to visit Badamtam during a period of great uncertainty and insecurity; the British owners of many of the tea gardens were feeling increasingly uneasy in post-independence India and thinking about returning to England.

It took many years of diligent work, but Gordon managed to form a family of companies, including a number of the tea estates in the Darjeeling area (Badamtam, Thurbo, the famed Margaret's Hope, and Castleton) and numerous other gardens in the Dooars region and across the border in Bangladesh. Though based in London, the Camellia Group put the management of the tea estates in the hands of the local nationals. Today, Camellia is one of the largest tea producers in the world, with estates in India and Bangladesh, and Kenya and Malawi in Africa.

To spend a few days at one of these estates is a life-changing experience. Badamtam, for example, is a rare place, with schooling for the children of the tea pickers, a hospital and health clinics, as well as community halls and temples in each of the major sectors of the estate where specific communities live. There one feels a palpable sense of belonging on the part of all stakeholders. Today all these tea estates have not only survived but are thriving, with the continued assurance of employment for thousands of workers and their families.

What Gordon wrote years ago as chairman of Camellia captures the essence of his business philosophy: "Above all we seek to be a company of genuine moral integrity and professionalism, with a real concern for the interests and welfare of our employees ... Inconvenient and costly though it may sometimes be, adherence to these principles wherever we operate is fundamental to our self-respect, inner strength, and long-term achievement." In this same report, he also wrote, "Nothing I have seen or experienced over forty years of professional life has led me to alter my view that a business can be run with a 'human face,' for the benefit not only of shareholders but equally for its employees, as well as general benefit of the societies and environment in which it works."[12]

Camellia exists not only to generate shareholder returns but also to ensure the continued employment of people whose welfare is inextricably linked with the fate of these tea estates. To do this, Gordon takes a long view of profits, with an attitude of custodianship rather than ownership. In a recent book on the Camellia Group, the well-known management guru Charles Handy affirms Gordon's approach:

> "As a commercial enterprise, profits are of necessity a high priority for Camellia, but never of ultimate importance. In many instances profits have been the by-product of careful long-term planning and execution rather than a specific aim in themselves. Similarly, its steady growth has not been the result of any obsessive need to be biggest or the best, but rather the outcome of the way the business is run. This approach is heavily influenced by Camellia's view of the concept of time and the nature of ownership."[13]

Over time, Gordon transferred his majority shares to a charitable entity, a foundation whose responsibilities include, in addition to continuing support of charitable activities in the tea estate regions, the guardianship of the culture, ethos, and management philosophy of Camellia. To sit on the board of this foundation has been one of the greatest honors of my life. Today, if there are parts of the world where thousands of tea workers can go to bed with the rare sense of security that their home, livelihood, and community will be there for a long time to come, this is due primarily to the fact that more than half a century ago, someone with a courageous heart brought conscious intention into managing these valuable assets with compassion. I had the good fortune to accompany Gordon on a visit to Badamtam Tea Estate in 2013, and was moved to see the deep affection the entire community feels for him. Camellia today has more than 73,000 employees worldwide, and even at the height of the global financial crisis the company brought healthy dividends to its shareholders.

Toward a more just and compassionate society

If there is one fundamental insight that social science has taught us, it's this: *Unless we change social structures and institutions, we cannot expect our society to change in any fundamental, enduring way.* So much suffering and unfairness is caused by structural conditions of our society, such as discrimination based on race, religion, gender, and sexual orientation. Not coincidentally, societies that have undergone fundamental structural changes since the Second World War are the ones where citizens now enjoy the highest degree of freedom, respect for individual rights, and dignity. Nothing captures the spirit of the postwar ethos better than the UN's Universal Declaration of Human Rights, which represents the first systematic global expression of basic standards for a civilized society's treatment of its citizens. Although this charter emerged directly from the experience of the war, I view it as a culmination of a longer history, perhaps going all the way back to the European Enlightenment. Together with democracy, the imperative to structure society on the basis of respect for fundamental human rights is Western civilization's greatest gift to humanity.

This UN charter also represents a landmark answer to the perennial question: What is the right balance between the welfare of the individual and that of the collective? By articulating the basic rights of the individual, which he or she enjoys by virtue of simply being human, universal human rights set clear boundaries that even the State—the collective—cannot cross, except under clearly defined circumstances. The charter declares that our default position as a society will be to trust the individual, a choice that has proved quite prophetic. Today, where there is respect for human rights, societies generally thrive, with citizens feeling safer, freer, and valued. Whether we look at the Soviet experiment or at today's more affluent Communist China, where there is no commitment to basic human rights, the State always treats its citizens with fear, suspicion, and oppression. This naturally gives rise to an inherently unstable system, where every critical expression from citizens is perceived by the State as a threat.

When compassion naturally arises in us in response to human suffering, it's the concrete individuality of the predicament that elicits our compassion—not some abstract idea of humanity, but the specific reality of suffering in front of us. However, when we make compassion our conscious intention for structuring our society, it's the idea of humanity and the alleviation of suffering that concerns us. In other words, compassion as an emotional response is passionate, personalized, and focused on the specific, while compassion as an outlook is dispassionate, depersonalized, and focused on the abstract, not unlike the blindfolded Justice. The individual recipient of justice could be anyone—you, me, white, black, Asiatic, religious, nonreligious, rich, poor; what matters is that he or she is a citizen with basic rights and dignity. At this level, justice and compassion, two fundamental components of our ethics, come together.

Buddhist thought also recognizes that compassion, in its most developed form, is not contingent upon the particulars of individual suffering. Compassion arises as our response to suffering, period; whose suffering it is should not matter. Shantideva puts it this way:

> Simply because it's suffering,
> it must be warded off.
> Why is any limitation put on this?
> No one disputes and questions
> why suffering should be prevented.
> If it must be prevented, all of it must be.
> If not, this goes for oneself as for everyone.[14]

The beauty of structural and institutional change is that the benefits are shared universally. Logically, anyone who is dedicated to compassion will also be committed to social change, not just personal transformation. People who work to promote social justice, respect for human rights, and greater democracy around the world are champions of compassion in action. This has nothing to do with bringing "inappropriate" Western values to non-Western parts of the world. Personally, I find the suggestion that values such as respect for basic human rights are somehow inappropriate in other parts of the world to be an insult to the people and cultures in those parts of the world. In the developed world too, including the West (where I live now), clearly many structural improvements are still needed to create a more equitable and compassionate society. The struggle is far from over. However, because of democracy, respect for human rights, and an independent judiciary and media, whenever the citizens so choose, we can change society to make it more caring, compassionate, and fair.

We cannot wait for our society to change; we must take the initiative to make change. A more compassionate world starts with individuals, people just like you and me. Hopefully, this book has helped you see that compassion isn't heroic; it's human. When we look, we can always find opportunities to express our compassionate side through kindness in our everyday life. The question is not whether I am compassionate; rather, the question is: Will I make the choice to express the more compassionate part of me? Whether we live our lives with compassion, whether we relate to ourselves, others, and the world around us from a place of compassion, understanding, and kindness is up to us. To me, this is also the most important spiritual question of human existence.

There is a saying in the Tibetan tradition that the best measure of our spiritual development is how we relate to death when our final day arrives. We are advised to be able to leave, when our time comes, if not with a sense of joy, at least with no remorse. Furthermore, we are told, naked awareness of our mortality can help us align our deepest aspirations and everyday actions. It can also bring a kind of brutal honesty—and courage—to our life. It leaves little room for false pretense or maintaining a facade, and reveals the fruitlessness of expending too much energy taking care of our ego. It's stark but, I have found, helpful advice.

When our time finally arrives, each one of us departs this world alone. We cannot take our wealth, fame, or even our education with us. What we can take are the thoughts and feelings of our last days. Have I made my life purposeful? Have I been loved? Have I loved and cared for others? Have I touched others' lives in meaningful ways? Have I brought joy into the lives of others? Has my existence mattered to other people's well-being? These are the questions that will occupy our mind as we approach our end.

In any case, these are the questions that should matter most to us as human beings, whose happiness and suffering are defined by our relationships with others. So why not start living our lives from this very moment as if they do? Why wait? There is no better time to start. Time always moves on. The Dalai Lama often reminds us that no force can stop time; but how we use our time, wisely and meaningfully or not, is up to us. For me, compassion is the key to a meaningful life. It is my sincere hope that some of the reflections and suggestions offered in this book may help you and others like you—*just like you*—to put compassion at the center of your life and see how it changes the world.

Acknowledgments

Buddhist philosophy recognizes that behind even a single event there are multiple causes and conditions and that we cannot know them all. So, as I sit down to write these lines to say "Thank you" to those who have helped make this book possible, I am acutely aware that I will miss many names.

First and foremost, I would like to thank His Holiness the Dalai Lama for his masterful leadership in promoting compassion in the world and for always showing us what it means to live it both in thought and in action. My late monastic teacher Kyabje Zemé Rinpoché tutored me in the rich Buddhist philosophical, psychological, and meditative traditions. Without having the presence of these two teachers in my life, I cannot imagine being able to write this book.

The Center for Compassion and Altruism and Education Research (CCARE) at Stanford University also figures significantly in the background of this book. Here, I express my appreciation to James R. Doty, the director of CCARE, for inviting me to be a founding member of the center and giving me the opportunity to develop what became the Compassion Cultivation Training (CCT). Margaret Cullen, Erika Rosenberg, and Kelly McGonigal—three remarkable teachers of psychology and meditation—made invaluable contributions to the program's further development as the first senior instructors of CCT. They were later joined by Monica Hanson and Leah Weiss. The Omidyar Network, through the HopeLab, generously supported the training of two cohorts of CCT instructors. Edward Harpin and Robert McClure established a robust presence of CCT at Sharp HealthCare in San Diego. Jeanne L. Tsai, Birgit Koopmann, Philippe R. Goldin, and Hooria Jazaieri at Stanford undertook scientific studies on the effects of CCT. I offer my deepest thanks to all of you, for without your active roles, CCT would not be where it is today.

I would like to thank my agent, Stephanie Tade, for her passionate belief in this book and for giving me the necessary courage to take it on. I thank Caroline Sutton, my publisher at Hudson Street Press, who has been most generous with her time, attention, and insights. Her critical comments on my two drafts kept me constantly striving for greater clarity and cohesion. I thank two other individuals who have been crucial in the writing of this book as well. Leah Weiss helped with the research and gathering of CCT instructors' stories, and carefully read my drafts at various stages. And I was fortunate to receive the help of Stephanie Higgs at the eleventh hour. By tightening the text yet relaxing the voice, sharpening the narratives, and making me fill the gaps, Stephanie helped bring something truly amazing to my final manuscript.

I am indebted to two close friends who read drafts at various stages and offered valuable feedback: K. C. Branscomb Kelley and Jas Elsner. It was in fact K.C. who, for several years, encouraged me to write a book for the general audience. I thank

Gordon Fox and Simon Turner for their contributions on the story of the Camellia Group of companies; Zara Houshmand for her help in editing part one of the book; and CCT course participants who shared their inspiring stories, which I have cited in the book. Two colleagues, Richard Davidson, a fellow board member of the Mind and Life Institute, and Brian Knutson, a colleague at Stanford University, kindly read the final manuscript and offered advice that helped sharpen my presentations of the scientific studies. While acknowledging their counsels, I take full responsibility for any shortcomings in my reading of science.

I would also like to acknowledge Nita Ing and the Ing Foundation for their generous patronage of the Institute of Tibetan Classics, which helped support part of my time during the writing. Last but not least, I thank my family. My daughters, Khando and Tara, dared me to share more aspects of my personal life with the reader. My wife, Sophie, patiently listened to each chapter as I wrote it, and her observations helped keep me on course. Her constant love and stabilizing presence are among my best karma.

Whatever good emerges from the creation of this book, through this, may each one of us experience the warmth, courage, and lasting joy of genuine compassion.

Notes

Introduction

1 These are biannual five-day dialogues between scientists from diverse fields and the Dalai Lama, which take place at his residence in Dharamsala, India. The proceedings of many of these conversations, which began in 1987, are available in various books. See www.mindandlife.org.

2 Frans de Waal, *Primates and Philosophers: How Morality Evolved*, edited by Stephen Macedo (Boston: Harvard University Press, 1998), 10. De Waal attributes this quote to American biologist and philosopher Michael Ghiselin.

3 Karen Armstrong, *Twelve Steps to a Compassionate Life* (New York: Alfred A. Knopf, 2010), 19.

4 For a review of scientific studies on compassion, including its evolutionary roots, see Jennifer L. Goetz, Dacher Keltner, and Emilia Simon-Thomas, "Compassion: An Evolutionary Analysis and Empirical Review," *Psychological Bulletin* 136, no. 3 (2010): 351–74.

5 One of the focuses of the Charter for Compassion movement initiated by Karen Armstrong, a noted author on world religions, is to encourage followers of the world's major religions to collectively adopt it.

6 See, for example, Paul Ekman, *Moving Toward Global Compassion* (San Francisco: Paul Ekman Group, 2014).

7 Some of the important findings of brain imaging studies on long-term meditators done at Richard Davidson's labs are reported in the following papers: Antoine Lutz, Laurence L. Greischar, Nancy B. Rawlings, Matthieu Ricard, and Richard J. Davidson, "Long-term Meditators Self-Induce High-Amplitude Gamma Synchrony During Mental Practice," *Proceedings of the National Academy of Sciences* 101, no. 46 (2004): 16369–73; J. A. Brefczynski-Lewis, A. Lutz, H. S. Schaefer, D. B. Levison, and R. J. Davidson, "Neural Correlates of Attentional Expertise in Long-term Meditation Practitioners," *Proceedings of the National Academy of Sciences* 104, no. 27 (2007): 11483–8; and Antoine Lutz, Julie Brefczynski-Lewis, Tom Johnstone, and Richard J. Davidson, "Regulation of the Neural Circuitry of Emotion by Compassion Meditation: Effects of Meditative Expertise," *PLoS One* 3, no. 3 (2008): e1897.

8 For a lucid presentation of mindfulness and its central practices from the creator of mindfulness-based stress reduction (MBSR), see Jon Kabat-Zinn, *Wherever You Go, There You Are: Mindfulness Meditation in Everyday Life* (New York: Hyperion, 1994).

9 Ralph Waldo Emerson, "Books," in *Society and Solitude* (Boston and New York: Fireside Edition, 1909). The full quote reads: "I do not hesitate to read all the books I have named, and all good books, in translations. What is really best in any book is translatable—any real insight or broad human sentiment."

10 Personal communication with Robert McClure, a psychotherapist and senior CCT instructor at Sharp HealthCare, in San Diego, California.

Chapter 1: The Best Kept Secret of Happiness

1 Alfred, Lord Tennyson, In Memoriam A. H. H. Canto 56.

2 Thomas Huxley, *Evolution and Ethics and Other Essays* (London:

Macmillan & Co, 1895), 199–200. For a succinct presentation of the influential Western views on selfishness as our defining nature and its early critics, see Frans de Waal, *Primates and Philosophers: How Morality Evolved*, ed. Stephen Macedo (Boston: Harvard University Press, 1998), 3–21.

3 Thomas Nagel, *The Possibility of Altruism* (New Jersey: Princeton University Press, 1970), 19. Nagel compares prudence to altruism and argues that prudence involves conceiving our present situation as merely a stage in a temporally extended life and caring about our future selves. Altruism, on the other hand, involves the conception of ourselves as merely one person among others and arises from our capacity to view ourselves both as *I* and as *someone* at the same time.

4 Daniel C. Batson's seminal publications on the topic include "Prosocial Motivation: Is It Ever Truly Altruistic?" *Advances in Experimental Social Psychology* 20 (1987): 65–122; *The Altruism Question: Toward a Social-Psychological Answer* (Mahwah, NJ: Lawrence Erlbaum Associates, 1997); and more recently *Altruism in Humans* (Oxford: Oxford University Press, 2011).

5 For two of the best representatives of this emerging understanding of human nature within science, see Elliott Sober and David Sloan Wilson, *Unto Others: The Evolution and Psychology of Unselfish Behavior* (Boston: Harvard University Press, 1998); and de Waal, *Primates and Philosophers*. See also Frans de Waal, *The Age of Empathy: Nature's Lessons for a Kinder Society* (New York: Broadway Books, 2010).

6 Greater Good, "What Is Compassion?" http://greatergood. berkeley.edu/topic/compassion/definition.

7 *Udanavarga*, a collection of aphorisms attributed to the Buddha. All translations from classical Buddhist and Tibetan sources in the book are mine unless otherwise stated.

8 This quote from Jean-Jacques Rousseau's *Emile* is cited in

Adam Phillips and Barbara Taylor, *On Kindness* (New York: Farrar, Straus and Giroux, 2009), 34.

9 Adam Smith, *The Theory of Moral Sentiments* (New York: Dover Philosophical Classics, 2006), 4.

10 Charles Darwin, "Moral Sense," in *The Descent of Man, and Selection in Relation to Sex Vol.1* (New Jersey: Princeton University Press, 1982 [1871]), 69.

11 There is a growing body of neuroscientific literature on the neuronal basis of empathy and how it implicates various brain regions. See, for example, S. D. Preston and F. B. de Waal. "Empathy: Its Ultimate and Proximate Bases," *Behavioral and Brain Sciences* 25 (2002): 1–72. For a review of current studies as well as a succinct presentation of the issues related to mapping empathy in the brain, see Boris C. Bernhardt and Tania Singer, "The Neural Basis of Empathy," *Annual Review of Neuroscience* 35 (2012): 1–23.

12 The results of their collaborative studies on children as well as nonhuman primates were published in Felix Warneken and Michael Tomasello, "The Roots of Human Altruism," *British Journal of Psychology* 100, no. 3 (2009): 455–71.

13 The results of the original study conducted on six-month-old infants in the New Haven, Conn., area were published in J. Kiley Hamlin, Karen Wynn, and Paul Bloom, "Social Evaluations by Preverbal Infants," *Nature* 450 (2007): 557–60.

14 Davidson makes this comparison between our natural capacity for language and compassion in his various talks when presenting his team's studies on the effects of compassion meditation.

15 Brandon J. Cosley, Shannon K. McCoy, Laura R. Saslow, and Elissa S. Epel, "Is Compassion for Others Stress Buffering? Consequences of Compassion and Social Support for Physiological Reactivity to Stress," *Journal of Experimental Social Psychology* 46, no. 5 (2010): 816–23.

16 See, for example, Kristin Layous, S. Katherine Nelson, Eva

Oberle, Kimberly A. Schonert-Reichl, and Sonja Lyubomirsky, "Kindness Counts: Prompting Prosocial Behavior in Preadolescents Boosts Peer Acceptance and Well-being," *PLoS One* 7, no. 12 (2012): e51380.

17 This study was first conducted under the leadership of Stanford psychologist Brian Knutson in 2008, and later replicated with brain imaging as well. The results of these studies are being prepared for publication.

18 This is a multiyear research project being undertaken at the Center for Mind and Brain, University of California, Davis, with the neuroscientist Clifford Saron as one of the principal investigators. For the findings related to the effect on telomerase, see T. L. Jacobs, E. S. Epel, J. Lin , E. H. Blackburn, O. M. Wolkowitz, D. A. Bridwell, A. P. Zanesco et al., "Intensive Meditation Training, Immune Cell Telomerase Activity, and Psychological Mediators," *Psychoneuroendocrinology* 36, no. 5 (2011): 664–81.

19 Jeremy P. Jamieson, Wendy Berry Mendes, and Matthew K. Nock, "Improving Acute Stress Responses: The Power of Reappraisal," *Current Directions in Psychological Science* 22, no. 1 (2013); 51–6.

20 A formal description of the study can be found at *http://news.uchicago.edu/article/2014/02/02/16/aaas-2014-loneliness-major-health-risk-older-adults*. See also Ian Sample, "Loneliness Twice as Unhealthy as Obesity for Older People, Study Finds," *Guardian*, February 16, 2014.

21 Miller McPherson, Lynn Smith-Lovin, and Matthew E. Brashears, "Social Isolation in America: Changes in Core Discussion Networks over Two Decades," *American Sociological Review* 71, no. 3 (2006): 353–75.

22 Christina R. Victor and A. Bowling, "A Longitudinal Analysis of Loneliness Among Older People in Great Britain," *Journal of Psychology* 146, no. 3 (2012): 313–31.

23 See, for example, Jonathan Haidt, "Elevation and the Positive

Psychology of Morality," in *Flourishing: Positive Psychology and the Life Well-Lived*, ed. C. L. M. Keyes and Jonathan Haidt (Washington, DC: American Psychological Association, 2003), 275–89.

24 Simone Schnall, Jean Roper, and Daniel M. T. Fessler, "Elevation Leads to Altruistic Behavior," *Psychological Science* 21, no. 3 (2010): 315–20.

Chapter 2: The Key to Self-AcceptancE

1 Jennifer Crocker and Laura E. Park, "The Costly Pursuit of Self-Esteem," *Psychological Bulletin* 130, no. 3 (2004): 392–414.

2 Personal communication with Edward Harpin, a pain psychologist, mindfulness trainer, and senior CCT instructor at Sharp HealthCare, in San Diego, California.

3 The discussions from this seminal conference on Buddhism and psychotherapy were published under the title *Worlds in Harmony: Dialogues on Compassionate Action* (Berkeley, CA: Parallax Press, 1992).

4 For a systematic presentation of Kristin Neff's framing of self-compassion as constituted by three key dimensions, see her "Self-Compassion: An Alternative Conceptualization of a Healthy Attitude Toward Oneself," *Self and Identity* 2 (2003): 85–101. For a book-length presentation of Neff's understanding of self-compassion and how to cultivate and enhance it, see her *Self-Compassion: Stop Beating Yourself Up and Leave Insecurity Behind* (New York: HarperCollins, 2011).

5 Kristin Neff, Kullaya Pisitsungkagarn, and Ya-Ping Hsieh, "Self-Compassion and Self-Construal in the United States, Thailand, and Taiwan," *Journal of Cross-Cultural Psychology* 39, no. 3 (2008): 267–85.

6 See, for example, Amanda Ripley, "Teacher, Leave Those Kids Alone," *Time*, September 25, 2011.

7 M. R. Leary, E. B. Tate, C. E. Adams, A. B. Allen, and J. Hancock,

"Self-Compassion and Reactions to Unpleasant Self-Relevant Events: The Implications of Treating Oneself Kindly," *Journal of Personality and Social Psychology* 92, no. 5 (2007): 887–904.

8 See, for example, Barbara Oakley, Ariel Knafo, Guruprasad Madhavan, and David Sloan Wilson, eds., *Pathological Altruism* (Oxford: Oxford University Press, 2011).

9 See, for example, Hazel Rose Markus and Alana Conner, *Clash! 8 Cultural Conflicts That Make Us Who We Are* (New York: Hudson Street Press, 2013).

Chapter 3: From Fear to Courage

1 See, for example, Paul Gilbert, Kristin McEwan, Marcela Matos, and Amanda Rivis, "Fears of Compassion: Development of Three Self-report Measures," *Psychology and Psychotherapy* 84, no. 3 (2011): 239–55.

2 Paul Gilbert, "Self-Criticism and Self-Warmth: An Imagery Study Exploring Their Relation to Depression," *Journal of Cognitive Psychotherapy* 20, no. 2 (2006): 183.

3 The representative thoughts indicating our fears related to compassion presented here have been adapted from the more extensive list found in Gilbert et al., "Fears of Compassion."

4 See, for example, Dalai Lama, *Beyond Religion: Ethics for a Whole World* (New York: Houghton Mifflin Harcourt, 2011), 68.

5 Personal communication with Robert McClure, psychotherapist and senior CCT instructor at Sharp HealthCare, in San Diego, California.

6 In the Oxford World Classics translation, Shantideva's verse reads, "Where is the hide to cover the whole world?/The wide world can be covered with hide enough for a pair of shoes alone." Shantideva, *The Bodhicaryavatara*, ed. Paul Williams, trans. Kate Crosby and Andrew Skilton (Oxford: Oxford University Press, 1995), 35.

7 As translated in Thomas Byrom, *The Dhammapa: The Sayings of the Buddha* (Vintage eBooks, 2012).

Chapter 4: From Compassion to Action

1 Personal communication with my colleague Leah Weiss, one of the senior instructors of the Stanford compassion training.

2 This quote is from *Udanavarga* (Collection of Aphorisms), attributed to the Buddha and translated from the Tibetan version of the text.

3 Personal communication with Edward Harpin, senior CCT instructor at Sharp HealthCare, in San Diego, California.

4 Quoted in Daniel Goleman, *Focus: The Hidden Driver of Excellence* (New York: Harper Collins, 2013), 258.

5 Jennifer Crocker and Amy Canevello, "Egosystem and Ecosystem: Motivational Perspectives on Caregiving," in *Moving Beyond Self-Interest: Perspectives from Evolutionary Biology, Neuroscience, and the Social Sciences, ed.* Stephanie L. Brown, R. Michael Brown, and Louis A. Penner (New York: Oxford University Press, 2012), 211–23.

6 Ibid., 214.

7 What I am referring to here as "Buddhist psychology" includes primarily the classical Buddhist discipline called *abhidharma* (literally "manifest knowledge"). Roughly, the *abhidharma* texts deal with the understanding of the structure and content of human experience, including the roles various emotions play in our experience of happiness and suffering. There is, however, another category of classical Buddhist knowledge known as *pramana*, which could be roughly characterized as the Buddhist equivalent of epistemology. The texts in that genre typically deal with questions that are the main purview of contemporary cognitive science.

8 For an excellent synthesis of the current scientific research on

motivation and its implications, see Reed W. Larson and Natalie Rusk, "Intrinsic Motivation and Positive Development," *Advances in Child Development and Behavior* 41 (2011): 89–130.

Chapter 5: Making Way for Compassion

1 Matthew A. Killingsworth and Daniel T. Gilbert, "A Wandering Mind Is an Unhappy Mind," *Science* 330, no. 6006 (2010): 932.

2 Harvard University, "Mind Is a Frequent, but Not Happy, Wanderer: People Spend Nearly Half Their Waking Hours Thinking About What Isn't Going On Around Them," *ScienceDaily*, November 12, 2010, http://www.sciencedaily.com/releases/2010/11/101111141759.htm.

3 See, for example, Daniel B. Levinson, Jonathan Smallwood, and Richard J. Davidson, "The Persistence of Thought: Evidence for a Role of Working Memory in the Maintenance of Task-Unrelated Thinking," *Psychological Science* 23, no. 4 (2012): 375–80.

4 See, for example, John Tierney, "Discovering the Virtues of a Wandering Mind," *New York Times*, June 28, 2010, http://www.nytimes.com/2010/06/29/science/29tier.html.

5 In a recent paper, a team of researchers on self wrote: "When objects and events are viewed through the eyes of the self, stimuli are no longer simply objective aspects of the world, but they typically become emotionally colored, and thereby more intimately related to one's sense of self." George Northoff, Alexander Heinzel, Moritz de Greck, Felix Bermpohl, Henrik Dobrowolny, and Jak Panksepp, "Self-Referential Processing in Our Brain—A Meta-analysis of Imaging Studies on the Self," *Neuroimage* 31, no. 1 (2006): 441. See also Seth J. Gillihan and Martha J. Farah, "Is Self Special? A Critical Review of Evidence from Experimental Psychology

and Cognitive Neuroscience," *Psychological Bulletin* 131, no. 1 (2005): 76–97.

6 T. D. Wilson, D. A. Reinhard, E. C. Westgate, D. T. Gilbert, N. Ellerbeck, C. Hahn, C. L. Brown, and A. Shaked, "Social Psychology. Just Think: The Challenges of a Disengaged Mind," *Science* 345, no. 6192 (2014): 75–7. For a review of this study and its relation to our contemporary digitally invasive lifestyle, see Kate Murphy, "No Time to Think," *New York Times*, July 25, 2014.

Chapter 6: Getting Unstuck

1 The Tibetan equivalent of this Sanskrit term is *jesu tsewa*, which literally means "to care after."

2 Personal communication with Robert McClure, psychotherapist and senior CCT instructor at Sharp HealthCare, in San Diego, California.

3 Amaravati Sangha, "Karaniya Metta Sutta: The Buddha's Words on Loving-Kindness," Access to Insight (Legacy Edition), November 2, 2013, http://www.accesstoinsight.org/tipitaka/kn/snp/snp.1.08.amar.html.

4 For a lucid presentation of loving-kindness meditation as studied by Fredrickson and her team, see Sharon Salzberg, *Loving-Kindness: The Revolutionary Art of Happiness* (Boston: Shambhala, 2002).

5 Barbara L. Fredrickson, Michael A. Cohn, Kimberly A. Coffey, Jolyn Pek, and Sandra M. Finkel, "Open Hearts Build Lives: Positive Emotions, Induced Through Loving-Kindness Meditation, Build Consequential Personal Resources," *Journal of Personality and Social Psychology* 95, no. 5 (2008): 1045–62.

6 Ibid., 1057.

7 B. E. Kok, K. A. Coffey, M. A. Cohn, L. I. Catalino, T. Vacharkulksemsuk, S. B. Algoe, M. Brantley, and B. L. Fredrickson, "How Positive Emotions Build Physical Health: Perceived Positive

Social Connections Account for the Upward Spiral Between Positive Emotions and Vagal Tone," *Psychological Science 24, no. 7* (2013): 1123–32.

8 Quoted in Maia Szalavitz, "The Biology of Kindness: How It Makes Us Happier and Healthier," *Time*, May 9, 2013.

9 Panchen Lobsang Chögyen, *Lama Chöpa* (Celebrating the Guru), a well-known Tibetan verse text.

10 See, for example, R. A. Emmons and M. E. McCullough, "Counting Blessings Versus Burdens: An Experimental Investigation of Gratitude and Subjective Well-being in Daily Life," *Journal of Personality and Social Psychology* 84, no. 2 (2010): 377–89; and R. A. Sansone and L. A. Sansone, "Gratitude and Well Being: The Benefits of Appreciation," *Psychiatry 7, no. 11* (2010): 18–22. For a review of scientific research on gratitude and its therapeutic effects, see R. A. Emmons and R. Stern, "Gratitude as a Psychotherapeutic Intervention," *Journal of Clinical Psychology* 69, no 8 (2013), 846–55.

11 Thupten Jinpa, trans., *Mind Training: The Great Collection* (Boston: Wisdom Publications, 2006), 301.

12 For an introduction to this Japanese meditation practice, see *Naikan: Gratitude, Grace, and the Japanese Art of Self-Reflection* (Berkeley, CA: Stone Bridge Press, 2001), by Gregg Krech, who is associated with the ToDo Institute, a Naikan education and retreat center in Vermont.

13 *The Bodhicaryavatara*, 6:21. The Oxford World Classics translation reads: "The virtue of suffering has no rival, since, from the shock it causes, intoxication falls away and there arises compassion for those in cycle of existence ..."

14 Desmond Tutu, *God Has a Dream: A Vision of Hope for Our Time* (New York: Doubleday, 2004), 37.

Chapter 7: "May I Be Happy"

1 For a comprehensive introduction to attachment theory, see M. Mikulincer and P. R. Shaver, *Attachment in Adulthood: Structure, Dynamics, and Change* (New York: Guilford Press, 2007).

2 For a review of these findings, see Paul Gilbert and Sue Procter, "Compassionate Mind Training for People with High Shame and Self-Criticism: Overview and Pilot Study of a Group Therapy Approach," *Clinical Psychology & Psychotherapy* 13, no. 6 (2006): 353–79.

3 Personal communication with Robert McClure, psychotherapist and senior CCT instructor at Sharp HealthCare, in San Diego, California.

4 On learning to distinguish between the language of observation and judgment, see Marshall B. Rosenberg, *Nonviolent Communication: A Language of Life* (Encinitas, CA: PuddleDancer Press, 2004), especially Chapter 3.

5 Tom Kelley and David Kelley, *Creative Confidence: Unleashing the Creative Potential Within Us All* (New York: Crown Press Business, 2014), especially the introduction and Chapter 2.

6 Rosenberg, *Nonviolent Communication*, 134.

7 *Ibid.*, 133.

8 Gilbert and Procter, "Compassionate Mind Training," 363.

9 John Makransky, *Awakening Through Love: Unveiling Your Deepest Goodness* (Boston: Wisdom Publications, 2007), 22. For those with theistic religious persuasions, the reflections offered in Desmond Tutu's book *God Has a Dream*, especially Chapter Three, "God Loves You as You Are," can be adapted as a powerful personal practice on self-acceptance and self-kindness (Desmond Tutu, *God Has a Dream: A Vision of Hope for Our Time* (New York: Doubleday, 2004)).

10 Personal communication with Margaret Cullen, a senior CCT and certified mindfulness instructor.

11 Personal communication with Leah Weiss, one of the senior instructors of the Stanford compassion training.

12 Personal communication with Margaret Cullen.

Chapter 8: "Just Like Me"

1 Kristen Renwick Monroe, *The Heart of Altruism: Perceptions of a Common Humanity* (Princeton, NJ: Princeton University Press, 1996).

2 Ibid., 105.

3 Ibid., 206

4 Ibid., 206.

5 Personal communication with Robert McClure, psychotherapist and senior CCT instructor at Sharp HealthCare, in San Diego, California.

6 Piercarlo Valdesolo and David DeSteno, "Synchrony and the Social Tuning of Compassion," *Emotion* 11, no. 2 (2011): 262–6.

7 David DeSteno, "Compassion Made Easy," *New York Times*, July 14, 2012.

8 Alexander Genevsky, Daniel Västfjäll, Paul Slovic, and Brian Knutson, "Neural Underpinnings of the Identifiable Victim Effect: Affect Shifts Preferences for Giving," *Journal of Neuroscience* 33, no. 43 (2013): 17188–96.

9 Personal communication with Leah Weiss, a senior instructor of the Stanford compassion training.

10 Personal communication with Robert McClure.

11 The Tibetan "mind training" refers to a genre of spiritual writings and their associated practices, which focus on training our mind and heart toward a more altruistic outlook and conduct. Two well-known texts of this class are *Eight Verses for Training the Mind* and *The Seven-Point Mind Training*. For an English translation of selected key mind-training texts, see Thupten Jinpa, trans., *Essential Mind Training* (Boston: Wisdom Publications, 2011).

12 For an example of how to apply life cycle analysis in everyday life and its social and environmental impact, see http://practicalaction.org/product-lifecycle-analysis.

13 As found in a letter from 1950 and quoted in the *New York Times,* March 29, 1972. A different version of the same quote is found in Alice Calaprice, *The New Quotable Einstein* (Princeton, NJ: Princeton University Press, 2005), 206.

14 For a concise and lucid presentation of tonglen practice by a contemporary Western Buddhist teacher, see Pema Chödrön, *The Places That Scare You: A Guide to Fearlessness in Difficult Times* (Boston: Shambhala, 2001), 70–78.

15 Personal communication with Robert McClure.

16 *The Bodhicaryavatara,* 8:104–6.

Chapter 9: Greater Well-being

1 Carol D. Ryff, "Happiness Is Everything, or Is It? Explorations on the Meaning of Psychological Well-being," *Journal of Personality and Social Psychology* 57, no. 6 (1989): 1069–81; Carol D. Ryff and Burton Singer, "The Contours of Positive Human Health," *Psychological Inquiry* 9, no. 1 (1998): 1–28.

2 Ryff, "Happiness Is Everything," 1072.

3 Personal communication with Edward Harpin, senior CCT instructor at Sharp HealthCare, in San Diego, California.

4 This study and its findings are cited in Daniel Gilbert, *Stumbling on Happiness* (New York: Alfred A. Knopf, 2006), Chapter 1. The findings of this study are formally presented by its authors, E. Langer and J. Rodin, in "The Effect of Choice and Enhanced Personal Responsibility for the Aged: A Field Experiment in an Institutional Setting," *Journal of Personality and Social Psychology* 34, no. 2 (1976): 191–8.

5 Anthony D. Ong, C. S. Bergeman, and Steven M. Boker, "Resilience Comes of Age: Defining Features in Later Adulthood," *Journal of Personality* 77, no. 6 (2009): 1782.

6 See, for example, B. L. Fredrickson, M. M. Tugade, C. E. Waugh, and G. R. Larkin, "What Good Are Positive Emotions in Crises? A Prospective Study of Resilience and Emotions Following Terrorist Attacks on the United States on September 11th, 2001," *Journal of Personality and Social Psychology* 84, no. 2 (2003): 365–76.

7 *The Bodhicaryavatara*, 6:10.

8 Hooria Jazaieri, Kelly McGonigal, Thupten Jinpa, James R. Doty, James J. Gross, and Philippe R. Goldin, "A Randomized Controlled Trial of Compassion Cultivation Training: Effects on Mindfulness, Affect, and Emotion Regulation," *Motivation and Emotion* 38, no. 1 (2014): 23–35. A study at Emory University of undergraduates participating in a six-week compassion training, similar to CCT, found reduction in subjective and physiological response to psychosocial stress. See Thaddeus W. W. Pace, Lobsang Tenzin Negi, Charles L. Raison, Daniel D. Adame, Steven P. Cole, Teresa I. Sivilli, Timothy D. Brown, and Michael J. Issa, "Effect of Compassion Meditation on Neuroendocrine, Innate Immune and Behavioral Responses to Psychosocial Stress," *Psychoneuroendocrinology* 34, no. 1 (2009): 87–98.

9 James J. Gross, "The Emerging Field of Emotion Regulation: An Integrative Review," *Review of General Psychology* 2, no. 3 (1998): 275.

10 Jazaieri et al., "A Randomized Controlled Trial," 25.

11 Ibid.

12 This line of thinking is cogently developed in, for example, Marc Hauser, *Moral Minds: How Nature Designed Our Universal Sense of Right and Wrong* (New York: Ecco Press, 2006). Although serious questions have been raised about the integrity of some of Hauser's experiments, I find the overall argument of the book compelling.

13 Dalai Lama, *Ethics for the New Millennium* (New York: Riverhead Books, 1999); and *Beyond Religion: Ethics for a Whole World* (New York: Houghton Mifflin Harcourt, 2011). I had the

privilege to assist the Dalai Lama in the writing of both of these important books.

Chapter 10: More Courage, Less Stress, Greater Freedom

1 Daniel Kahneman, *Thinking, Fast and Slow* (New York: Farrar, Straus and Giroux, 2011).

2 Charles H. Duhigg, *The Power of Habit: Why We Do What We Do in Life and Business* (New York: Random House, 2012), 12.

3 For an engaging account of the important scientific discovery of neuroplasticity and its implications for healing and personal transformation, see Norman Doidge, *The Brain That Changes Itself: Stories of Personal Triumph from the Frontiers of Brain Science* (New York: Penguin Books, 2007).

4 Personal communication with Margaret Cullen, a senior CCT and certified mindfulness instructor.

5 For an insightful account of contemporary scientific findings on how our emotions affect our thoughts and life, see Richard J. Davidson and Sharon Begley, *The Emotional Life of Your Brain: How Its Unique Patterns Affect How You Think, Feel, and Live—And How You Can Change Them* (New York: Hudson Street Press, 2012).

6 Chapter 6 of Shantideva's *The Way of the Bodhisattva* contains a masterful presentation of the psychology of forbearance and its cultivation. For a detailed exposition of this important chapter, see Dalai Lama, *Healing Anger: The Power of Patience from a Buddhist Perspective, trans.* Thupten Jinpa (Ithaca, NY: Snow Lion, 1997).

Chapter 11: The Power of One

1 From John Donne's poem *Devotions upon Emergent Occasions*. The full line reads, "No man is an island, entire of itself."

2 Personal communication. Matthieu Ricard has recently

published, in French, a major book on altruism titled *Plaidoyer pour l'altruisme: La force de la bienveillance.*

3 This internal study was conducted by Janina L. Scarlet, measuring the effects of compassion training using, among others, Job Satisfaction Scale, Interpersonal Conflict Scale, and Self-Compassion Scale. The courses were taught by Robert McClure and Edward Harpin, two prominent members of Sharp HealthCare, who were both trained as senior CCT instructors. Source: Personal communication.

4 For more information on social and emotional learning (SEL) and its key components, see http://www.casel.org/social-and-emotional-learning. For a recent review of the impact of SEL programs, see J. A. Durlak, R. P. Weissberg, A. B. Dymnicki, R. D. Taylor, and K. B. Schellinger, "The Impact of Enhancing Students' Social and Emotional Learning: A Meta-analysis of School-Based Universal Interventions," *Child Development* 82, no. 1 (2011): 405–32.

5 L. Fook, S. B. Goldberg, L. Pinger, and R. J. Davidson, "Promoting Prosocial Behavior and Self-Regulatory Skills in Preschool Children Through a Mindfulness-Based Kindness Curriculum," *Development Psychology*, 2014 November 10 (Epub ahead of print).

6 Other sources for the Zone de Paix program include adaptations of basic Buddhist-derived breathing and visualization practices, and Sura Hart and Victoria Kindle Hodson's NVC-based program for schools titled *The No-Fault Classroom: Tools to Resolve Conflict & Foster Relationship Intelligence* (Encinitas, CA: PuddleDancer Press, 2008). In 2010 Tara Wilke, PhD joined to teach the Zone de Paix program and has helped develop it further with Sophie.

7 Marshall B. Rosenberg, *Nonviolent Communication: A Language of Life* (Encinitas, CA: PuddleDancer Press, 2004), 52.

8 Dalai Lama, *Beyond Religion: Ethics for a Whole World* (New York: Houghton Mifflin Harcourt, 2011), Chapter 1.

9 For a description of this research on compassion in an organizational setting, visit www.thecompassionlab.com.

10 Lawrence Mishel and Alyssa Davis, "CEO Pay Continues to Rise as Typical Workers Are Paid Less," Economic Policy Institute, Issue Brief #380, June 12, 2014.

11 See, for example, Thomas Piketty, *Capital in the Twenty-first Century* (Cambridge, MA: Harvard University Press, 2014). For an excellent review by an economics Nobel laureate, identifying and evaluating some of the key theses of Piketty's book, see Paul Krugman, "The Piketty Panic," *New York Times*, April 25, 2014; and "Is Piketty All Wrong?" *New York Times*, May 24, 2014.

12 As quoted in Michael Manton, *Camellia: The Lawrie Inheritance* (Sevenoaks, Kent: Camellia plc, 2000).

13 Charles Handy, *Camellia: A Very Different Company*. In-house publication of the Camellia Foundation, 2013.

14 *The Bodhicaryavatara*, 8:102.